How to develop a
TALENT FOR TRAINING

For a complete list of Management Books 2000 titles,
visit our web-site on http://www.mb2000.com

How to develop a
TALENT FOR TRAINING

A very practical guide for trainers

Sandy Leong

2000

First published in 2004 by Management Books 2000 Ltd ·

Forge House, Limes Road
Kemble, Cirencester
Gloucestershire, GL7 6AD, UK
Tel: 0044 (0) 1285 771441
Fax: 0044 (0) 1285 771055
E-mail: mb2000@btconnect.com
Web: www.mb2000.com

Printed and bound in Great Britain by Digital Books Logistics of Peterborough

British Library Cataloguing in Publication Data is available

ISBN 1-85252-468-5

Contents

Introduction

How to develop a Talent for Training is a book packed with information and practical tips for anyone who wants to work as a trainer or as a teacher with adults; or for any trainers or teachers who want to improve their training skills. It doesn't matter what the subject area is on which you will be training, all the information and tips in this book, will apply.

If you are someone who is new to the field of training, reading this book will increase your confidence. It will give you the knowledge and skills to behave like an expert trainer who has got everything under control, whilst appearing relaxed and approachable. If you are already working in the training field, it will be a useful reference guide for you.

This book contains the theories around training, so that you will feel better equipped and more knowledgeable. But its main focus is really practical tips to make your training sessions run smoothly, and making the participants who attend your courses feel happy and comfortable, and therefore better able to learn.

Sandy Leong has run training courses for many years, on a wide range of subjects. Her favourite area is working with those wishing to become trainers, or those new to training who want to improve their training skills. She has been in the education field almost all her working life, beginning as a teacher, before moving into training and development. She has assisted many individuals to improve their training practices, and encouraged many new to training to enjoy it and develop and grow in the role.

1
What Makes a Good Trainer?

... can anyone do it?

Do you remember the last time that you were a participant on a training course? How did you feel when the trainer opened his or her mouth to speak? Did time go into slow motion, and did the chairs become harder as you struggled to absorb what the trainer was saying? Or were you instantly interested? Then amazed that it was already time for the coffee break.

What actually makes the difference between trainers who are good, and those who are either mediocre or poor? It is easy to differentiate between the abilities of different trainers when you are a participant on a training course, but how do you make sure that you are in the good to excellent category when you are the trainer, being judged by the participants?

Enthusiasm

The most important ingredient that separates good trainers from others is ENTHUSIASM. Being enthusiastic is the key element to being an effective trainer and to running successful training courses. All the other things that are going to be covered in this chapter are necessary, but without enthusiasm, you will never be viewed as a good trainer.

Pause for a moment and think about the type of person with whom you would prefer to spend the day. Would it be an enthusiastic person, who has a zest for life, or would you choose to spend time with some one for whom life seems a bit of a struggle? Most of us would prefer the former. Participants want to be lead by someone who is full of life and passionate about their subject – not someone who looks as if they would rather be somewhere else. You have to be enthusiastic, whether you feel like it or not.

Sometimes when you are running training courses every day, it can be difficult to be enthusiastic all of the time. Difficult, but not impossible. To display enthusiasm (real or not) you have to consider how you are coming across to your audience (the participants). Enthusiasm comes from your tone of voice and your body language, not the words that you actually say.

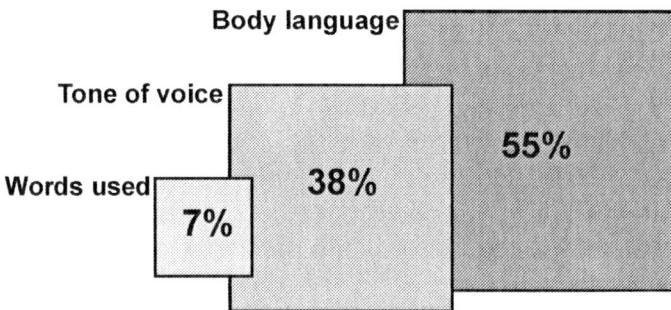

Figure 1 – Communication model

The communications model (figure 1) shows that in face-to-face communication 55% of the message of what you are trying to convey is given by your body language; 38% of the message comes from the tone of voice that you use and only 7% of the message is conveyed by the actual words that you are saying.

To appear enthusiastic, you need to use a positive, encouraging tone of voice, and a natural but energetic style of body language. There is no point in just saying that the subject fascinates you and that you are pleased to be working with the group. You have to demonstrate those facts. If there is any incongruence between the words that you use and the tone of voice and the body language you are using when you say them, it is always the tone and body language which will be believed. Simply saying that you are enjoying yourself is not enough; you have to demonstrate the fact.

What makes a good trainer?

Enthusiasm

Confidence

Control

Being relaxed

Sense of humour

Knowing your subject

Good communications skills

If you are enthusiastic (real or manufactured) you can get the group interested in the subject that you are talking about, and on your side. Enthusiasm is contagious, and as a trainer, it's your job to spread it around. When you don't feel enthusiastic, which, let's face it, is quite possible, then you can't afford to let it show. Very few people are filled with enthusiasm every single day they go to work. Unfortunately, as a trainer, you can't have 'off' days.

Someone in the room has to be filled with enthusiasm, and it has to be the trainer. There will be days when you are feeling tired, fed up or just wish that you were sitting on a white beach, in the sun. Too bad; you have to fake it. You need to develop your acting skills, and make sure that they are good enough for the participants not to see through them and discover the miserable trainer lurking beneath your bright exterior.

Confidence

Being enthusiastic will help you to appear CONFIDENT. If you are confident, the participants will be confident to learn. Participants want to feel that they are in a safe and relaxed environment. The trainer can create this by appearing to be confident.

In order to appear confident, you should never go for the sympathy vote from participants, no matter how unsure you are feeling. Maybe you don't feel very well, maybe you are using new material, and don't feel comfortable with it. It doesn't matter how you feel you can't let it show. If you try to get a group on your side by telling them that you don't feel very well, or that you have had to stand in for some one else at the last minute and because of that you aren't very well prepared – it won't work. Participants divide into two types of people, the sympathetic and the harsh. The sympathetic will respond to a call for sympathy by becoming anxious for you, willing you to succeed. The harsh will wonder what you are doing setting yourself up as a trainer if you aren't properly prepared. Whichever group the participants fall into, they won't be feeling comfortable and therefore their learning may suffer.

To make sure that you are coming across as confident, you need to be aware of the body language that you are using and get rid of any that makes you look unsure of yourself. The classic body language leakage areas for trainers are fiddling with marker pens, standing on one leg, and shuffling papers. To appear confident (even when you don't feel it) you have to minimise these habits and develop stronger, more powerful gestures.

Control

If you are enthusiastic and confident (or at least appear to be) you will be able to keep the group on track much more easily. Any group of participants need to feel that the trainer is in control of both the group processes, and the material that is being taught, to be able to learn comfortably. Keeping CONTROL has various elements to it; You must make sure that everyone feels safe enough to contribute to the group; that everyone is clear about what they are doing and why they are doing it during the training process; making sure that you stick to the programme timings, or negotiating any changes with the group; making sure that all the necessary training resources are available when needed, and most importantly, ensuring that the refreshments are suitable for all the participants and that they arrive on time. If you get all that right, the participants will be able to learn in an environment which feels safe and comfortable, and they will be willing to come back for more.

Being relaxed

So you are enthusiastic, confident, and in control. The next area to think about is appearing RELAXED. Who said this was easy? The last thing participants want is a nervous, edgy, trainer, or one who over compensates, and who appears to be arrogant and full of their own self-importance. Part of being confident is appearing to be relaxed. To be relaxed, you need to be confident with your materials and preparation. If you are working with new or less familiar material, that can be difficult, so you need to develop strategies to help yourself.

Sense of humour

You appear to be confidant, to be in control, but also to be relaxed and enthusiastic – What about having a SENSE OF HUMOUR? Using your sense of humour, and making things fun, helps participants to learn. A little bit of fooling around (if you can pull it off) helps to break up the learning, and can go down very well. You need to make sure that the humour is appropriate to the group. It's also better to laugh at yourself than at anyone in the group. If you really think that you can't fool around and crack jokes, don't try. If it doesn't come naturally, it's not to be recommended.

Knowing the subject

Another thing that makes a good trainer almost goes without saying. A good trainer KNOWS THE SUBJECT, and knows it well. It is not advisable to stand up in front of a group if you don't know much about the subject area that you are supposed to be covering. If you have flown close to the wind on the odd occasion, maybe at a meeting or somewhere else, you will know that it doesn't make you feel relaxed and confident. Not when you are hoping that no one will see through your lack of knowledge and catch you out at any moment. When you are delivering a subject, you need to know more about it than you are actually intending to deliver to the group of participants. You never know when there might be a question from a participant that needs to be answered. Not being able to answer a participant's question is a quick way of losing credibility. It's okay to say that you don't know occasionally, but not too often.

Although you need to know more about your subject than you are going to deliver, you also need to know when to stop. There is nothing worse than an enthusiastic trainer who goes on and on. A good trainer makes sure that they are delivering the information that is appropriate to the group with whom they are working. That is both what they want and what they need to know. Save anything else for the next course, or for that clever question from that one participant. Then you will be able to wow them by knowing the answer.

Trainers also need to stick to the point. Don't get carried away and start to deviate until even you don't know where you started from and where you were intending to go Be clear and succinct; occasionally tell short anecdotes to illustrate a point, and then move on to the next point. Imagine that everyone has to take notes from what you are saying, and think about how easy or difficult it would be to do that from your method of delivery. Summarising what you have said at the end of each section is a good technique. It clarifies learning, and helps anyone who may have dozed off momentarily (or longer), to stay on track.

Good communication skills

It goes without saying that a trainer needs to have GOOD COMMUNICATION SKILLS. You need to be able to get the subject across and to portray yourself well. Communicating divides into two broad areas, transmitting (talking) and receiving (listening). Obviously, you have to be good at transmitting, otherwise you're not going to get the message across. But you also need to be good at receiving (listening) or you won't understand what is happening for either the individual participants or the group with whom you are working.

As a trainer, the areas of communication that you need to be aware of are:

- **Clarity**: Participants need to be able to understand what you are saying, and be able to see the logic of where you are starting from and where you are going.

- **Pitch**: Participants need to be able to hear you. You don't want to boom across the room, deafening people, but you have to make sure that you are loud enough for everyone to hear you comfortably. If participants can't hear the trainer, then they switch off, write tomorrow's to do list, test their artistic ability in doodling or become disruptive.

- **Tone and pace**: You need to use different tones of voice to keep participants interested in what you are saying. Using a monotone will send people to sleep fairly rapidly. Varying the tone and pace of your delivery is a must. Remember that 38% of the message that you are conveying is understood via the tone of voice. So you have to work hard at it.

- **Language**: Good trainers need to make sure that they use language that is appropriate to the group. Don't be condescending or patronising. Check out what people know and don't know. If you want or need to use jargon, first check out that everybody understands it. Never assume everyone understands it, because often people won't ask, but will sit either confused or fed up, either way not learning.

- **Listening and observing**: You need to listen carefully to what participants are really saying or asking. There are two types of listening, 'listening waiting to speak', and 'active listening'. The first type is exactly what it says, waiting for the speaker to shut up so that you can say what you want to say. Consequently you are not giving them your full attention. Active listening is consciously attending to what the speaker is saying in order to ensure that you understand what they are really telling you or asking you. That is not just listening to the words that the participant is saying but listening for the tone of voice being used, checking out the context in which the words are being said and trying to second guess the speaker's emotions.

   You should use active listening to ensure that you can accurately answer any question or queries. You also need to pick up on any fears and concerns that participants may have. It is much better to try and deal with these as they appear, rather than carrying on serenely only to find a group of unhappy participants, half way through the training course.

Whilst you are training, you are constantly trying to read what's happening in the group. You should be watching out for clues in participants' body language, and their communications with others, to try and ascertain how the participants are feeling. You want to know whether they are engaged in the learning process, or if they are bored, and getting fidgety. You can't be a mind reader, but you can try your best to work out what is happening, and match your delivery style and content to needs of the participants.

As mentioned earlier in this chapter, a good trainer should be well prepared. Once the preparation is done, it frees you to be enthusiastic, confident, and relaxed before you undertake any training. You should have thought about the following areas as part of your preparation:

● **The organisation**: What type of organisation will you be working for? Is it formal or informal? What is the organisational culture? Are there likely to be hidden agendas? What systems are in place for the learning to be evaluated?

● **The participants**: what is it that they want from the training? What do they know already? How willing are they to learn?

● **The content**: Does what you have planned match the organisations objectives? Does it match the participant's objectives? What training techniques will be best or acceptable?

● **The material**: Do you need to make any changes to your material? Are the case studies and other exercises that you intend to use appropriate to the group? Is there enough material prepared? That doesn't necessarily have to be on paper, it can be in your head, so that you can be flexible and responsive to the group. Even if you have researched the group well, things can be different on the day.

If you work on all the points covered in this chapter, you have a good chance of becoming an excellent trainer rather than just an average one. Training is a competitive area for getting work. Average trainers don't get repeat work that often. It's like being on stage; actors are remembered for their last performance. So are trainers.

2
The Necessary Bits

... training theory that you need to know

Having an understanding of the theories behind both the learning and the training is necessary to become an effective trainer. But, more importantly is the ability to be able to relate these theories to the training situation. A good trainer uses his or her knowledge of the theories in a practical way, to assist in the development of both the training programmes and the training materials, to enable participants to learn.

To develop useful training programmes you need to be familiar with the training cycle. This is important because it gives you a structure to follow when developing and carrying out a training intervention.

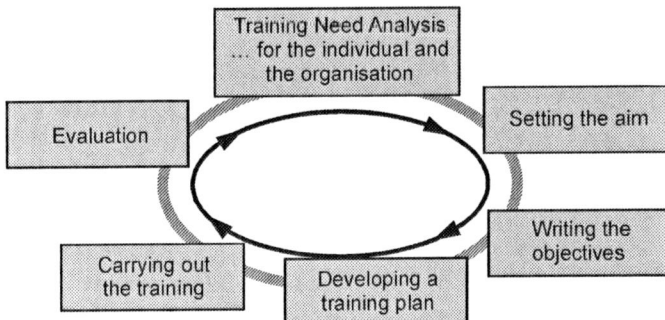

Training Need Analysis ... for the individual and the organisation

Evaluation

Setting the aim

Carrying out the training

Developing a training plan

Writing the objectives

Figure 2 – The training cycle

Training need analysis

The training cycle begins with a **training needs analysis** (TNA for short). Conducting a training needs analysis should ensure that the training to be delivered will be effective for both the learner's development and will assist the organisation to move closer towards its goals. Obviously, this should be carried out prior to any training being planned or delivered. There are several different models for conducting a training needs analysis. However all training needs analyses are carried out under three headings – **knowledge, skills and attitudes**. (This is often referred to as the '**k.s.a.**'). When you are conducting a training needs analysis, you should be identifying what knowledge, what skills and what attitudes people need to be able to do the job in question, to the required standard.

Once this has been documented, the next stage in the process is to identify what knowledge, skills and attitudes the person who is to be trained actually possesses, and to what level. This is then matched against what they actually need, to be able to do the job effectively. The resulting difference between the k.s.a. that the person already has and what he or she needs to do the job effectively, is called the **training gap**. This is the area that the training will cover, to ensure that the learners are up to the required standards to do the job effectively.

All different types of training needs analysis follow the same formula. It is usually the detail in which they are carried out that makes them different. For example, to carry out a training needs analysis for a manual type of job, the tasks that make up the components of the job could be broken down into fine detail, and each area looked at in terms of what knowledge, skills and attitudes would be required to successfully carry out each component of the job. To undertake a similar process for a management role would be very difficult, as you would be dealing with the broader brush strokes of managing people.

To identify the knowledge, skills and attitudes that a person needs to be able to do the job to the required standards, you should look at the paperwork that already exists in the organisation. The best place to start is with the **job description** and **person(nel) specification**. The job description describes the job to be done and the personnel specification describes the person best suited to do the job.

Other useful paperwork that is usually available in organisations is the **strategic** or **business plan** that is used to show how the organisation is intending to develop. This would therefore indicate what training may be necessary to develop staff to move the organisation forward.

In addition to the two most obvious pieces of paperwork are any other policy documents that the organisation has developed. These could be customer service standards, IT policies, equal opportunities policy and any others that are relevant to the day-to-day work of the staff group in question.

These documents will not only identify the knowledge and skills that staff will need to do the job to the required standard, but will also highlight the set of attitudes that staff need to display when they are carrying out the work.

To match up an individual against the knowledge, skills and attitudes required to do the job, you should look into what existing structures there are within the organisation, in order to be able to assess each individual.

On a formal level, you could use the outcomes of **supervision sessions** or **appraisals**. Or you could gather **feedback** from the managers of the individual staff members. You could also conduct face-to-face **interviews** with the staff in question to discuss their level of knowledge and skills and attitudes in relation to their jobs.

21

On an informal basis you could use your own observations of situations involving the staff in question. For example, it is quite easy to observe if receptionists or other front line staff are working to the standards written in the organisation's customer standards or policy document. This can be done by frequently walking through the organisation's reception area and watching how the staff are dealing with customers.

Any training needs that you perceive through this informal method should then be moved into a more formal arena, perhaps by calling the staff in question to a meeting to discuss training needs and the job standards that are required of them. This is meant to be a positive move to improve service and staff training and should not be conducted as if you were trying to catch people out.

Training packages that have been developed from a good training needs analysis should be much more effective than others that have not come from a TNA, as the *real* training needs have been identified. Staff who are asked or ordered to undertake training for which they can see no need, are less likely to learn, and you the trainer will certainly not have a room full of happy bunnies. All experienced trainers know that a room full of happy bunnies is much more preferable to a room full of unhappy bunnies.

Aims

Once you have conducted the training needs analysis, the next step is to develop from it a set of **aims and objectives** for the training that is going to be carried out. It may be at this stage that you as the trainer are involved in the process, and have not been involved in the training needs analysis which may have been carried out by someone else in the organisation. Or in fact you may be a freelance trainer and have been called in after the aims and objectives have been written, to design and deliver the training.

The scope of the training needs analysis will reflect how many aims and objectives will need to be written for the training in question. Each discrete piece of training will require its own aim and set of objectives. So, if you are working on one piece of training, for one staff group, you will have one aim and one set of objectives. If you are working with different staff groups and on different subject areas, you will have as many aims and sets of objectives as staff groups and subject areas.

An aim is identified as the 'purpose' for the training. It is a good way of summing up the training, and is what is often used in the publicity 'blurb' for a training course. For example, for a course that is to develop the training skills for staff who are not currently involved in the delivery of training, the aim might be, *to develop training skills for staff who wish to move into a training role.*

Objectives

When the aim has been written, the next stage is to write a set of objectives for the training. Training objectives are a precise statement of what participants will learn as a result of the training. The learning may result in new knowledge, new skills and new attitudes or feelings and therefore personal growth. Training objectives are usually referred to as **learning outcomes.**

Learning outcomes should be specific, measurable, achievable, related and time bound. They should be **SMART**. This is the acronym usually used when referring to objectives. As a trainer you should give your objectives the 'SMART' test, to check that you have really thought about them. Woolly objectives can lead to woolly training.

For example: The *aim* for a piece of training might be:

... to be able to run better meetings

The *learning outcomes* that you write to follow on from this aim could be something like the following (although they would come from your training needs analysis and relate directly to this group of learners needs).

Example objectives: (for a training course on developing effective meetings)

By the end of the training participants will: • understand what makes an effective meeting • have identified and discussed common problems of meeting behaviour • have practised bringing in and shutting out skills • ... and so on

Learning outcomes should be written using active and unambiguous language. They enable the trainer to be clear about the exact learning they are trying to achieve for the group that they are training. This includes the depth within the subject area to which they need to be working. This is whether they are working with a group of beginners on the subject in question, or are working with those who are more advanced in their work practices.

Particular attention should be paid to the active verb (usually the first words) of the learning outcome. For example, (will have) identified, practised or (will) understand – these words will give the trainer an indication of the level to which they are working. Obviously 'will understand' is a much tougher learning outcome than 'will have discussed', or 'identified'. 'Have identified' is probably compiling a list of areas thought of by the participants; 'understand' is a more in-depth exercise that requires you, the trainer, to check out whether the participants actually do understand the concept or information.

To give learning outcomes the 'SMART' test you need to check the following.

SMART

Specific

Measurable

Attainable

Related

Timebound

- **Are the learning outcomes specific?** If you wrote them, is the language used very tight and not ambiguous when you read it again, or when it is read by someone else if they are going to undertake the training?

- **Are the learning outcomes measurable?** That is, could you really measure whether the participants have actually learnt what they set out to learn. This can be a really good test of how well the learning outcomes have been thought through when they were written. To be able to 'test' what participants have learnt, you have to be very clear about what they *should have* learnt.

- **Are the learning outcomes achievable?** That is, can the participants that you are working with, in the time available achieve the learning outcomes. This includes thinking about whether the participants have the ability to undertake training at this level. Have they got the literacy, numeracy or language skills that will be required to fully understand the subject area that is going to be delivered on the training course? Have the participants enough prior experience or knowledge on the subject to be learnt to make sense of the

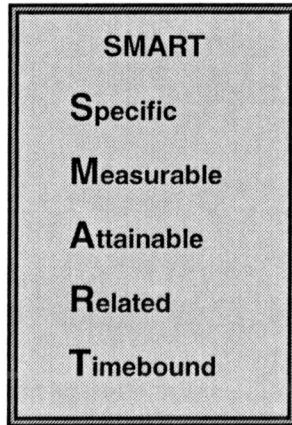

learning, or do they need to undertake some other preparatory study or work before they get to this point in their development.

- **Are the learning outcomes related to each other?** The learning outcomes should sit together in a cohesive way. If they don't, then maybe you have got more than one training course and should be looking to dividing them up.

- **Are the learning outcomes time-bound?** That is, when will the learning be complete? Learning outcomes are usually time-bound because of the way that they are written. They are usually written starting with the sentence, *by the end of the training participants ...*

Training plan

Once you have written the aim and objectives or learning outcomes from the training needs analysis, the next stage in training cycle is to write a training plan A training plan usually covers a period of twelve months. It may not be your responsibility to write a training plan, if you are only involved from the training delivery angle. However, someone in the organisation should have produced a training plan. This is produced once a year and would normally follow the annual appraisals. It is a well thought out plan of how the organisation is going to meet its training needs for the coming year.

A training plan usually sets out the aims and objectives for each training area, and each staff group that is going to be covered in the coming year. It also sets out what learning methods will be used to ensure that the learning is met, as there are many ways of developing staff other than sending them on a training course.

It would also cover the timing of each training intervention and who is to be responsible for it, and the budget or resources available for each area. The four areas of development covered in a training plan are:

- **induction** training for new staff
- **on-going skills and knowledge development** for existing staff
- **specific training** that will be required during that year, for example, any new changes in legislation or the introduction of new systems into the organisation
- and lastly **training for change** – this area would cover staff whose contracts are finishing or who are about to be made redundant.

The training plan should be a comprehensive document that plans ahead for staff development in an organised fashion, rather than training being a knee-jerk reaction to a problem. It can also motivate staff, if they can see progression for themselves and are able to engage in personal development.

Delivery

Once this is all sorted out, then you will be in a strong position to deliver top quality training, which participants want to attend, because they can see the purpose and the benefits to themselves. More on this later.

Evaluation

After the training, it is necessary to conduct an evaluation. Evaluation of training works on two areas – the evaluation of the learning and the evaluation of the training. Organisations and trainers often only evaluate the training. This is done immediately after a training course, with what are affectionately known as the 'happy sheets'. They are called happy sheets, because that is often about the only information that comes from them. The findings from these happy sheets or evaluation forms, usually tell you if the participants were 'happy' with the training course; whether they enjoyed being there and liked the trainer; what they thought of the venue and the lunch and refreshments. These are all valid points that you need to know. But it is not evaluating the learning. In fact it is difficult – if not impossible – to evaluate the learning until participants have had an opportunity to put it into practice when they get back to their workplace, or their everyday lives.

Climate

The training cycle deals with the more administrative side of training. It gives the trainer a sequence of events to follow when they are planning training. As trainers, it is necessary to plan the training well to ensure that participants learn as much as possible from the training situation that they are put into. Once the participants are engaged in the training intervention, it is the responsibility of the trainer to develop a learning climate. They need to be able to learn in a atmosphere that promotes and encourages learning and self development. This is obviously very important in assisting the successful learning outcomes for the participants.

Developing a positive climate in the training room, in which adults want to learn, is mainly the responsibility of the trainer. Adults, indeed anyone, learn best when they want to learn and they are encouraged to meet their own needs. If the learning on offer can be explained in terms of the adults' own needs and they can make or are helped to make the connections between what they are learning and how useful it will be to them, and how it builds onto their past experiences, then you are half way towards developing a positive learning climate on your training courses.

As trainers, you often see people who come on to your training courses for just a short time, sometimes only for the duration of the training course. This can be as short a length of time as a day or even a morning or an afternoon. You have to quickly establish a rapport with them to make them feel at ease.

To do this, it is necessary to be welcoming and approachable. So, if you possibly can, be near the door of the training room when participants are arriving to attend one of your training courses. Welcome participants to the training event, and guide them to their seat, or at least to a seat. Try to introduce them to the participant next to whom they are sitting. If you know something about each person, you can go a little further in your introductions and tell each participant a bit about the other one. You should not divulge anything too personal to the other participant, but something that could start a conversation between them. The sort of thing you might say is that she comes from the same area or works in a similar job.

Respond to any questions participants might have for you. It could be as simple as where the toilets are, or whether smoking is permitted, or more complex, maybe relating to the course content. Give them enough information, but don't get caught up in a long discussion with one participant. What you really need to be doing, in order to create that positive climate you are working towards, is to play the cocktail party host at this time, or perhaps acting out the functions of an air hostess or air steward, directing passengers to their seats, making them feel comfortable and smoothing any concerns or ruffled feathers.

This is a good time to check out any special needs that participants may have. You may have been alerted to these in some pre-course correspondence. If you have, identify the participants and, if it is appropriate, have a quiet word with them about their particular needs, for example, if they have a slight hearing or visual impairment they may want to sit near the front of the room.

You can make sure that this happens and you can reassure them before the training begins that you are aware of their needs and that you will take it into account when you move people into small groups, or when you are talking to the whole group.

Maybe their special need is a particular dietary requirement. It is good to tell them that you are aware of this and have it organised. It is easy to forget how something that perhaps doesn't seem very important, can make some participants anxious. If you can relieve participants of these types of worries, it will help to build a positive learning climate more quickly.

The room in which they are working also affects participants' willingness and capacity to learn. The size of the room and the amount of light that the windows let in can make a difference to how participants feel. Some training rooms don't even have windows; if you find yourself in that type of room, you are going to have to work much harder to make participants feel comfortable.

The degree of comfort of the room will also make a difference to participants' energy levels. This can be particularly evident in the afternoon sessions on training courses. The session straight after lunch is fondly known as the graveyard shift by most trainers. This is because it can be very difficult to motivate a sleepy bunch of participants in that session.

The degree of comfort in the room is important to how sleepy or uncomfortable participants might feel. Too much comfort and they will be falling asleep, too little comfort and they will want to leave by mid-morning.

So make sure that the room is set up with chairs that are comfortable to sit on for long periods of time, without having that cosy armchair feel to them; that there are tables for participants to rest on whilst they write, when they are needed, or when they get into small groups to work on an exercise when having a table available would make it easier to do the exercise. The simple rule is never give participants an opportunity to disengage with the learning process, especially if these things are in your control.

To make sure that participants are learning, you need to ensure that you take them all the way around the experiential learning cycle. Completing the experiential learning cycle is essential and it is your responsibility as the trainer.

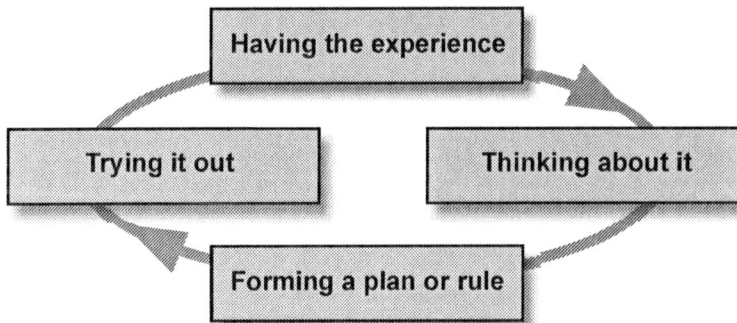

Figure 3 – Experiential learning cycle

The experiential learning cycle consists of four stages:

1. **Having the experience:** This is the stage when the learners try something out – that is, they experience something at first hand.

2. **Thinking about it:** The learners think about or discusses what happened when they were 'having the experience'

3. **Forming a plan or a rule:** The learners conclude from what they have experienced and thought about at stage two. They now form some general principles about what should happen

4. **Trying it out:** This is when the learners try out the learning. Often the learning becomes absorbed into the learner's behaviour at this stage.

A role-play exercise is a good example of how you can take participants around the experiential learning cycle. For the first stage, the participants engage in a role-play exercise; for the second stage, they think about and discuss what happened in the role play. Stage three occurs when they pull out the learning that has taken place and begin to form some general principles. At the final stage, the participants would undertake another role-play exercise trying out the new principles that they have found from going around the learning cycle.

As learners go through a continuous cycle of experiencing, thinking about the experience, putting these thoughts into general principles and then trying it out, they are learning. This is really what training is all about. Learning is about a personal change in behaviour. These changes work on three levels.

- The first one is a change to their level of knowledge.

- This in turn should cause a change in the way the person thinks, which is demonstrated in learners questioning their past ways of 'doing things'

- Lastly, a change in the way that they 'do' things in the future.

Another important issue in developing a learning climate is considering how different participants learn. Individuals have different learning styles. Some people like to learn by doing or having the experience. They like trying out new things and having new experiences. They don't mind taking risks. Some people learn best by watching other people do something. They don't like to be rushed into things. They like to sort things out before they act. Some people learn best when they can see the whole picture of where the learning fits in with other things. They can find learning difficult or frustrating if they are given only fragments and not the whole picture. The other type of learners learn best when they can see a practical reason and application for the learning.

No style is better or worse than another. There is not one style to which to aspire. Learners come in all shapes and sizes. Therefore it follows that learners will enter the learning cycle at different points, depending on their learning style. These are natural tendencies, which mean that some people learn better in different situations from others. So you need to use different training techniques to make sure that you engage all the different learning styles that participants bring to a learning situation. Some training techniques suit some learning styles better than others, and therefore will suit some participants more than others. The answer to this is to vary the training techniques that you use on your training courses, working on the principle that you can't please all of the people all of the time but you can please some of the people some of the time.

3
Understanding Training Techniques

... which method should you use?

Once the aim and the learning outcomes for the training course have been written, the next consideration for the trainer is how to put the actual content of the training course together. One of the most important, and sometimes most puzzling, questions for a trainer planning a training course is 'what training techniques will best achieve the stated learning objectives of the training?'

When planning a training course, the areas to be considered in deciding on which training technique to use are the actual *learning outcomes* for the training programme. You need to think carefully about what you actually want and need the participants to learn. Then you need to consider the participants' attitudes to the training, or at least what you think their attitudes might be when they arrive on the training course. Will they be happy and comfortable to 'try things out', perhaps take a risk of two, or will they require a safe environment where they can learn in a non-threatening way?

Also consider the different *learning styles* that could be present in the group of participants that you will have on the training course. Using different training techniques will allow participants with different learning styles to keep engaged in the training process, working on the principle that you can't please everyone all the time, but you can please some of the people some of the time.

WHICH TRAINING TECHNIQUE?

It depends on:

- **the learning outcomes**

- **different learning styles**

- **size of group**

- **participants' expectations**

On a more practical level, the *size of the group* with which you are going to work will make a difference to which training techniques that you chose to use. Some training techniques work best with small groups and vice versa. Some techniques just won't work at all if the size of the group is not suitable.

With all these constraints in mind, the training techniques (i.e. the vehicle for the learning) needs to be chosen carefully. Some training techniques are explained below; to use the range of techniques effectively, you need to understand how they work, and the advantages and disadvantages of each method.

Role Play

Role play is not usually a favourite activity with some participants on training courses. However, using a role play activity allows participants to experience real life situations in a protected and risk free environment. Because of this, it can be a powerful training technique to use, with the right subject area. When participants tell you that they don't like role-play exercises, it is often because they have experienced role-plays that have been poorly set up and run by the trainer. You may be able to overcome some objections if you do not use the phrase 'role play', but call the session a participation exercise or some such.

Trainers use role-play because it is a versatile learning tool that can be used in many different ways. The standard way of running a role play exercise is to get participants to work in pairs, sometimes with the addition of a third person who is an observer to what is happening in the exercise. Each person in the 'pair' is given a 'role' to play, during the exercise. These roles can be scripted, they can explain to the participants the type of person that they are supposed to be 'playing' during the exercise, or the participants could be asked to play themselves, during the role-play.

To set up a role-play exercise, the situation should be explained in detail, briefing participants on what the learning outcomes are for the session. Adults are usually much more willing to take part in an exercise if they know why they are doing it.

● They should be told what role each person will be playing, and given details about those roles, either verbal or written down.

● They need to be given time to think about how they are going to portray themselves in these roles. This is so that they can get into playing these roles as soon as the exercise begins and not waste time thinking about the role whilst they are trying to do the exercise.

● They should also be told what the timing is going to be for the exercise

● Lastly, they should be told what methods are to be used to take feedback after the session and what feedback you will be asking for them to give to you.

The role-play techniques should only be used when there is enough time in the training course to both set up the exercise very clearly and in enough detail, so that all the participants understand exactly what they should be doing and why they should be doing it *and* when there will be time to debrief from the session. That is to discuss all the learning, positive and negative that has come out of the participants doing the exercise, and give participants the time to 'de-role' from the roles that they have been playing. This is very important and participants should be given the time to talk about how they felt playing those roles. This sort of exercise can trigger baggage from the past that participants thought that they had dealt with, but can resurface during a difficult or powerful role-play exercise.

It is also advisable not to embark on using role play exercises at the beginning of a training course, when participants don't know each other too well, and therefore will feel less comfortable about exposing their thoughts and feelings in front of other participants. Not only will participants not be very happy about being asked to undertake the exercise, the quality and depth to which the exercise is carried out will be poor and therefore you might not achieve the required learning.

Advantages
The advantages of using this technique is that it really is a very powerful technique for getting participants to really feel and understand what could be happening for 'real' people who are facing the situations that you have asked them to play out in the exercise.

Disadvantages
The disadvantages are that many participants do have real aversions to role-play and feel reluctant to take part. Therefore you have to work very hard to generate and maintain participants' enthusiasm. The reason for doing the

exercise must be clearly understood by everybody or the participants' reluctance to carry out the exercise will show, either in the form of purposely not doing the exercise well or by getting the giggles and sabotaging it. Also, role plays do take a long time to set up, run, debrief and de-role. Never be tempted to use this technique on a training course if you feel that you are short of time.

Case Studies

Case studies are a really useful training technique because they can be used for so many different situations on a training course. A case study is a presentation of a specific incident, or incidents, usually with the relevant background information that participants need to make sense of the incident. It should be a situation that participants may have had to face in the past or may have to face in the future.

When selecting or writing a case study, you should consider how the case study will meet the learning objectives that have been set for the training course; whether the content of the case study is relevant both to the training course and to the participants who will be attending; and that the case study is easy to understand and does not need too much explanation because of its complexity.

When you are setting up a case study exercise with a group of participants, you should initially explain the reason why they are doing the exercise and the learning that is to come out of it. The case study should be written up and each participant given his or her own copy. Copies should be given out once you have explained what they are going to do and how they are going to do it. Don't give it out first, as the participants will immediately lose interest in what you are saying and begin reading the case study, as if it was breaking news headlines. Consequently they won't know what you want them to do, when you ask them to start the exercise.

So, go through the case study with the whole group and give them instructions on how long the exercise will last and what feedback you want from it at the end of the session. Also, tell the participants how you want the feedback to be presented, so that it will enable them to make the appropriate notes during the course of the exercise. Then move them into the small groups in which they will be working and only then give out the actual case study. Ask them all to read it before they begin to discuss it.

Advantages

The advantage of using the case study technique is that it is extremely versatile, and case studies can be written to suit the learning that is to take place. They also emulate reality and are therefore usually of more interest to participants as they can see how they can use the learning that will come out of the exercise.

Disadvantages

The disadvantages are that they can only be two dimensional and participants will sometimes feel the need to have more information about the 'characters' in the case study situation. It is always a fine balance between giving enough details in the case study to enable participants to understand what is going on, and not overloading the case study with details, which then take the participants a long time to develop their collective understanding of the issues posed. If the case study does not appear relevant to the group's issues or experiences, then they might not be interested or might be unwilling to make any connections between the issues being presented and their own issues.

Syndicate Groups

This training technique is one of the mainstays of training activity. Most trainers spend a lot of course time getting participants into groups and giving them something to discuss. A syndicate group is the term used to describe a sub group of the main group, which is given a specific task to do. The tasks are usually a case study exercise, a set of questions to answer or a statement to explore. The group have to discuss whatever they have been asked to do and prepare to report back their findings or answers to the main group.

When dividing the main group into syndicate groups ready for the task, you can divide the group at random, participants can be asked to self-select or you can pre-select the groups yourself. Which method you use will depend on the group itself and the task that you are going to ask them to carry out.

Advantages

The advantages of using syndicate groups are that it enables participants to get to know each other better, when working more closely with each other in small groups. It can keep up the energy level of the group, just by the sheer fact of getting participants to leave their seats and move around the training room. Also they get an opportunity to interact with different members of the group and hear their views about the subject in more detail, than if the training was all carried out in the large group. It also gives the shy or more reserved participants an opportunity to speak, in a situation which isn't as threatening to them as speaking in front of a large group.

Disadvantages

The disadvantages are that some participants actually seem to get irritated by having to physically move around the training room. Usually these are the ones that spread all their things out either around themselves or in front of themselves, and feel the need to move them to wherever they are in the training room. Sometimes the mix within the syndicate groups does not work so well and consequently the task isn't done so well. It can be a tedious technique if overused – that is, when the training only moves between input, syndicate groups and feedback from the groups.

Ideas Shower

An ideas shower is an outpouring of ideas from the participants, related to the area or problem under discussion. It is done to identify different ideas; to consider as many aspects of a problem as possible; or to act as a trigger for the group's discussion.

When setting up an ideas shower (often also called a brainstorming session), you should explain the process and the rule of the ideas shower to the participants. The rule is very simple but it is important that it should be adhered to. This is that every suggestion or idea that a participant makes has to be written on the flipchart or whatever, exactly as the participant has said it. It doesn't matter whether it appears to be relevant or even make sense at this stage in the exercise. There should be no censorship or discussion of what is being called out by the participants. Ideally, to avoid people thinking in lists and therefore not using real lateral thinking, the words should be written at random on the sheet rather than in columns or lines.

When the group has exhausted all its ideas, then it is time to move onto the next stage in the exercise. An ideas shower should always be sorted or ordered in some way, so that it makes sense to the participants. What you actually do with the ideas shower in terms of sorting it will depend on the learning objectives for the session. The options include; getting participants to discuss each thought or idea that has been written on the flipchart and disregard any ideas that do not make sense or don't fit in, or with which the group disagree. This should be done with coloured marker pens to group and sort the ideas. If the ideas are initially written on large post-it notes, then the business or ordering or discarding is made much easier. The items can be re-positioned or blocked to create groups of concepts or actions.

Advantages

The advantages of using an ideas shower is that it is a quick method for generating ideas from a group. It can be lively and fun, involving every one. It can also be a quick test of a group's reaction to the subject matter.

Disadvantages

The disadvantages are that if you have a quiet group it can sometimes be difficult to start the ideas flowing and the exorcise can be dominated by the louder members of the group. Conversely, some participants can opt out of the process. Lastly, if a contentious idea goes on to the flip chart it can be difficult to stop the group discussing it before the exercise has finished, which is obviously not a good idea.

Simulations

A simulation is a training activity designed to reflect reality. These can include role-plays, in-tray exercises or any other learning experience that has a real life aspect integrated into it. The learning comes from the participants' own experience in the activity and not always from the content.

Depending on what the simulation exercise is, it will need setting up accordingly. However there are areas of common ground for all simulations.

● You need to explain what the learning outcomes are for the exercise.

● You must give enough detail about who the participants will be during the exercise. Will they be playing themselves or are you going to give them roles to take on? If you are going to ask the participants to take on roles then you need to give them enough details about these roles so that they can easily imagine who they are to play.

● Explain 'where' are they going to be doing the exercise. Usually they will *actually* be doing the exercise in one of the training rooms or maybe outside, but where are they *pretending* that they are doing the exercise. Again you need to give them as much detail as possible so it makes it easy for them to imagine the setting. If it is at all possible, it is good to provide some props to help the atmosphere along a little.

● Then there is information about 'when' are they doing it. This is about what time of day, or what time of year are they pretending it is, when they undertake the exercise.

● And of course they need to be very clearly told how they should be carrying out the exercise, and how they are going to report back the learning that comes out of undertaking the exercise, maybe for them personally and collectively for the group with whom they have been working.

A stimulation exercise should only be planned into a training course when you know that you have plenty of time in which to run it and debrief from it. As it can take some time to set up to get participants to feel comfortable with what they are being asked to do, especially if they are being asked to take on different roles.

Advantages

The advantages of using simulation exercises is that, if they are well thought out, they closely emulate real life and therefore can be a powerful learning experience for participants with a great deal of both personal and group learning coming from undertaking the exercise. They can also be very interactive and great fun in which to take part.

Disadvantages

The disadvantages are that participants can sometimes resist taking on other roles and not be too happy about taking part. Skilful setting up of the exercises can usually alleviate this attitude. If the setting up of the simulation exercise is not well done, that is, usually the participants haven't been given enough detail or the detail hasn't been put across in a logical or easily understandable way, the participants are more likely to resist the exercise. Setting up a simulation exercise can be quite difficult and needs to be very well thought out.

Games

A game is a training technique that is governed by rules, has a competitive element and therefore usually results in winners and losers. Games do not usually reflect reality. The learning that comes from experiencing the game and the discussion that follows of what happened in the game are where the learning usually comes from, rather than the actual content.

Games are a versatile learning tool that can be used in several ways. There are many different types of games, which can be used as training tools; from the common family or playground games such as snakes and ladders or a trivial pursuits type of quiz game, to the outdoor type of challenges.

When setting up any game, the rules must be explained very clearly to the participants – one group of participants getting the rules wrong can sabotage the learning outcomes for that group. If there has been a competitive angle between the small groups, you will find yourself refereeing the game and how it was undertaken rather than discussing the learning outcomes at the end of the session.

The participants must understand why they are taking part in the game and understand what the learning outcomes are meant to be. Then they will be more willing to take part in the exercise. As games often don't simulate reality or can seem to have nothing to do with participants' working life or personal development, having them understanding why they are being asked to take part in the exercise is crucial.

Advantages

The advantage of using games on training courses is that it is a way of ensuring high participation in the training and hopefully participants will feel that they are having fun. It can get participants to interact with each other quickly and gives everyone a common experience, which can lead to the group bonding together more quickly. It can also change the pace of a training session – if you have had a session that is heavy on input, using a game can change the pace and revive interest and energy.

Disadvantages

The disadvantages are that some participants may be reluctant to take part in games. For some people, anything that appears to be of the party games type can make them instantly shut down. Some games may be too physical for some participants. It is therefore wise, if you have a game of the physical sort to either check it out with participants before they come on the course, or have a gentler back-up game if it seems to you that some of the participants would really struggle to take part in the exercise. There is a subtle difference between a challenge and something that may give your participants a heart attack.

4

The Minefield of Opening a Training Session

... starting with impact

The way you open a training session is very important. It sets the tone and atmosphere for the training. It gives participants some clues to how the session is going to run; whether it is going to be fun and interesting or not, and if it is going to be relevant to them as individuals. At this point, they start to make their minds up about whether they actually 'like' you as a person and a trainer. A great deal hinges on how you begin. So you have to get it right.

At the beginning of a training event, the trainer is expected to take the lead and get things moving. If this role is not carried out effectively participants will quickly lose confidence in the trainer's ability.

Start with impact

The way you open a training session should be positive, geared to getting participants thinking about the session and most of all grab their attention. It is best to stand up to deliver your introductory welcome. When standing, it is easier to look enthusiastic and welcoming. Sitting down can give a more downbeat impression. It is also more difficult to get people's attention when you are sitting down, especially if they are talking to each other.

So, stand up, deliver a bright and cheery good morning, good afternoon or good evening. Say who you are – your name, the company you work for and a little bit about yourself. Just a little bit! People don't want to hear your life story or how clever you are. What they want to know is that you are up for the job ahead. Reeling off a long list of credentials doesn't necessarily make you the right person for the job. So, keep your introduction brief and to the point. Try and focus what you are going to say to the group with whom you are about to start training. For example, 'I have worked with organisations like yours on this subject area' or 'I have worked in this type of organisation for over 10 years.'

The impression you want to give is that:

- you are enthusiastic and friendly
- it's going to be interesting to work with you today
- you know plenty about the subject
- you have had some real life experience of it
- you are in control.

If the group feels you are up for the job and that you are in control, they can relax and learn. They won't have to worry about whether things will go according to plan or start to fall apart.

Don't ever start a session by asking for a vote of sympathy, even if you feel that you need it. Never open a session by saying something negative. It starts the training off on a downbeat note. This makes participants feel either anxious for you and therefore uncomfortable or makes them wonder why you are the trainer? So, even if you are feeling a little unsure of your material, have a raging headache or toothache or just nearly crashed your car coming up the motorway, be positive, when you begin. Of course you need to continue to be positive all through the training, not just at the beginning.

Administrative and domestic arrangements

Once you introduced yourself, run through the administrative and domestic arrangements. Explain to the group what to do in the event of a fire, including where the fire exits and fire assembly points are located. You will have had to make sure you know exactly where they are placed. This is not a time to be vague. It is advisable to have arrived early enough before you are due to start the training to actually check these out. Often the notices in training rooms, giving this information are not all that clear if you are not familiar with the building. Tell the group where the toilets are situated. Not only the ones nearest to the training room, but any others a little further way, in case of congestion during break times. Explain what times the breaks will be taken and how long they will last; where tea/coffee/water can be found at the breaks and the arrangements for lunch.

Next, go rapidly through the course programme. It makes participants feel more comfortable if they know what is going to happen and when it is going to happen. By going through the course programme in more detail than what was written to be circulated to participants prior to the training event, explaining how the learning will be achieved, as you go through it gives participants more ownership of the learning. It allows them to relax into it and helps to create that positive learning climate that you are always working towards.

Ground rules for working together

Another area to be considered at the beginning of a training course is whether to set, or get the group to set, ground rules for working together. This is an important decision when working with any group. The decision whether to work with ground rules or not should be based on whether having them or conversely not having them will assist or hinder the learning process.

On the negative side, mentioning ground rules can turn people off as they feel that they may be forced to expose more of their private views, thoughts and ideas than they may want to disclose. This can set up resistance from the beginning of the session. On the positive side ground rules can be useful to set a group on to a constructive and positive way of working together. They are also useful to refer back to if things get a bit out of hand at any point in the training session. You should never just go through the motion of setting ground rules, because you always do it. You will find that the group is likely to do exactly the same and then ignore them.

The minimum ground rule you would be looking to agree with a lot of groups is one on confidentiality. That is, anything that is discussed in the training room stays confidential to that group of people. This ground rule is particularly useful when working in-house with a group who may wish to discuss the behaviour of colleagues or managers, in relation to a training exercise. This rule also applies to the trainer. Taking confidences shared in a training session and discussing them with other people – maybe a participant's manager – is not professional.

The areas usually covered by ground rules are:

Participation
There is an agreement that everyone will make an attempt

to participate in the group discussions, recognising some people will feel more comfortable talking in small group than in the large group.

Responsibility

Individuals should take responsibility for their own learning. They will need to listen; ask questions for clarification or for more information. They need to recognise that it is pointless sitting through something that they don't understand and then moaning about the lack of clarity or their confusion after the training session, when nothing can be changed.

Openness

Participants need to be honest about what they think and feel during the training. There is an expectation on them as individuals to share their thoughts and opinions, relevant to what is being discussed.

Sensitivity

Acknowledge that different people have had different experiences and will have different ideas and opinions which we should all respect, even if we don't agree with them. So an agreement should be made to listen to what other people have to say and if we don't agree with it to challenge what has been said, not to attack the individual.

Timekeeping and smoking

These can be sensitive areas. They are also the ones that can cause the most problems. One or two individuals being constantly late back from breaks can be difficult for both the participants and the trainer. Get the group to agree that they will adhere to the times of the breaks and come back on time. If you do this, then you have to make sure that you hit the breaks on time – no over-running – and you always start back again on time. Smoking can be an issue in a training session. You will need to agree when and where smoking is permitted. Never in the training room. Make sure you know where smoking is permitted in the building and then you can direct smokers to this area at break times. Smokers can often take longer at break times if they have to walk to the smoking area. So make sure you either extend the breaks by five minutes for everyone, to give the smokers a chance to get there and back in the time given, but also so that the non-smokers are not left waiting for the others to come back after every break.

Icebreaker exercise

When you have introduced yourself, told participants about the domestic and any administrative arrangements, gone through the programme and maybe set some ground rules, it is time to get participants to introduce themselves to the rest of the group. By using an icebreaking exercise, you can help participants feel more at ease with a group of strangers, or people they don't know very well.

An icebreaker exercise enables participants to start getting to know each other, by learning each other's names and something about each other. The right icebreaker can help to create the atmosphere you want in the group. You might want to use an exercise that gets people talking freely about themselves or one that will be fun and help people to relax and enjoy themselves. You might decide to use an icebreaker that makes people move around to get some energy into the room.

An icebreaker also gives the trainer an opportunity to weigh up the group. Are they chatty and ready to be friendly with each other? Are they quiet and reserved? Do they look as if they actually want to be attending the training, or do they look as if they have been sent by their managers? How co-operative are they?

Deciding which icebreaker to use can be left until you are faced with the group. It best to have a couple in mind and the resources ready to run them prepared and with you. Once you have had an opportunity to see the group and talk to them as they are coming in to the training room, you can decide which one to use. With experience, you can get a feel for a group fairly quickly and therefore make a more informed decision about which icebreaker to use. The next chapter describes some of the most effective icebreakers in detail.

CHOOSING AN ICEBREAKER

It depends on:

- **the size of the group**
- **participants' expectations**
- **length of the course**
- **subject area**
- **yourself as a trainer**

You can just look at some groups and guess that a certain type of icebreaker could go down like a lead balloon. The sort of things you are looking for are; is the group talking to each other readily or are they all sitting in silence. If they are chatting already, then it's probably going to be easier to get them involved and talking. However, they may have already introduced themselves to each other, or at least to the people next to whom they are sitting; or are they all sitting in silence, reading the literature you have provided and are not really appearing at this moment as if they are going to be a bundle of fun.

It is this sort of behaviour that will influence the decision on which icebreaker to choose. The other factors to take into account when choosing an icebreaker are:

The size of the group

The size of the group you are working with has a direct correlation on how long the icebreaker will take to run. With a large group you would need to run a shorter, more succinct icebreaker, giving each person less time to contribute. With a smaller group you can choose to give each participant more time to participate. The size of the group also influences the style of the icebreaker you might choose. A 'creeping death' type of icebreaker – that is the one where you start at one end of the group and ask everyone, in turn, to contribute something – can live up to its name and feel dreadful for groups larger than eight participants. Those at the beginning are relived to get their turn over and those in the middle and end wait for theirs in dread.

The expectations of the participants

Participants bring with them different expectations of the learning situation, often depending on their previous experiences of similar situations. If participants are expecting a formal session and you run a lively icebreaker exercise, they may not feel too comfortable. If you then go on to run the training in a formal way, they may be left wondering what the icebreaker was all about.

The length of the training course

An icebreaker exercise can be guaranteed to take longer than you expected. If you have a group of twelve participants and they all speak for about one minute, that will be twelve minutes gone, plus the time it took you to set up the exercise, plus the extra time for the more chatty or long winded participants. You should therefore have allowed twenty minutes for the exercise. If you are running a short, say two-hour, session, then quite a percentage of the time has gone already. You need to work out the balance between the group needing to know each other and the amount of content you need to get through. Of course, if you are running a week-long residential programme, then it is quite feasible to spend one hour running an icebreaker exercise. There is also a greater need for participants to get to know each other, as they will be spending a lot of time together.

The subject area of the course

Ideally an icebreaker should start people thinking about the course content. It should serve two purposes, as an introduction for the participants to each other and to the trainer, and a lead into the content of the training. Sometimes the latter can be difficult to accomplish. If you are using an icebreaker exercise that is not related to the course content, then you should explain this to the participants. By telling them that it is not related to the subject area you are going to cover, but is only a method of participants getting to know each other, it will save people sitting wondering what the connection was to the training. Or it will stop them resisting the exercise because they can see no point to it.

Yourself as a trainer

When you are setting up an icebreaker exercise, you need to feel comfortable with what you are going to ask the participants to do. If you feel either unsure of how the exercise might work or a bit uncomfortable with what you are asking participants to do, then it will show. If participants pick up that you are not too sure about what you are asking them to do, then there may be some one or even more people who decide that they are not going to take part in the exercise. Not a happy state of affairs for the beginning of a training session. So, if your icebreaker exercise consists of getting everyone to stand on one leg, hop around the room, whilst making chicken noises, you need the personality to be able to pull it off! Not that this is a particularly good idea, even if you have the strength of personality!

Setting up an icebreaker

Once you have decided which icebreaker exercise you are going to use, you need to be clear on how you will introduce it and set it up. Setting up an icebreaker needs plenty of energy from the trainer. So, when you are introducing it, always stand up. This gives you more of a presence. Use a very enthusiastic tone of voice, to convince the participants that what you are asking them to do is going to be enjoyable and useful. Be very clear with your instructions. Make sure that everybody in the room knows exactly what is expected of them. Explain to participants, what you want them to do: who you want then to do it with: where you want them to do it and what will happen at the end of the exercise. Then recap on the instructions you have just given to ensure that no-one has missed any part of them.

What you want them to do

When you are setting up an icebreaker exercise, you need to tell participants exactly what you want them to do and why you want them to do it. An example could be, a training course for participants who wish to develop their skills as trainers, on this course, setting up a simple icebreaker, you might say, 'Discuss with your partner your current involvement in training, or if you aren't currently involved in training then discuss what area or areas you would like to be involved.'

You should always give an opt-out option when you are asking participants to discuss a topic, unless you are absolutely certain that, in this case, everybody is involved in training of some sort. You don't want to embarrass anyone or alienate them from the training so early on in the session. It is also useful to tell participants what you don't want them to discuss, to try and keep them on the right track and avoid them wasting time. For example, you might say, don't go into detail about your organisation, we will be able to find out more about peoples' organisations as we go through the course.

Who you want them to do it with

One of the most difficult decisions for participant on a training course can be to decide whom to choose when they are asked to work in pairs or small groups. Who do they choose? Often participants will go for the easy option and just talk to the person sitting next to them. This doesn't get much energy into the room. Also they might have told that person all the information you are now asking them to share, whilst they were chatting waiting for you to start the session. So, give people a reason for choosing someone. The old favourite of someone you don't know always works well, unless, of course you have a group that all know each other.

Try something a bit different, like choosing someone with the same eye/hair colour, the same colour shoes. Anything that is a non-threatening way of getting people into pairs, threes or small groups. To get people moving, you will have to help, by getting into the group and asking questions like, do you know this person? Would you like to work with her or him. Or, to one person, what colour eyes have you got? To another, the same question. Both blue – then how about working together?

Often no one wants to be the first person in the group to stand up. By standing in the middle of the group yourself, you make the first participant to stand up the second person standing. If you help participants in their choices, it helps relax the atmosphere for what can be a seemingly simple process but one that can be difficult for some new groups. It also speeds up the process of getting into pairs or groups and therefore wastes less time.

If asking people to work in pairs when you have an odd number of participants, your linking with the odd one will show your willingness to participate on equal terms and will add to your credibility if you share the sort of information you are asking everyone else to provide.

59

Where you want it to happen

This is the air hostess or air steward bit for the trainer. You need to get people moving into pairs or groups and sitting in different parts of the room. Maybe you want to get them to move away from the tables to enable them to sit together in small groups so they are all able to see each other and talk more comfortably. Direct each pair or group to where you want them to be, using exaggerated body language, (hence the reference to the air hostess or air steward, particularly when they show you where the emergency exits are situated). Left alone at this point, participants will often try and talk to each other down the length of a table, thus making it difficult for those at either end to join in.

How long have you got

Make sure participants are clear about the timing of the icebreaker. Tell them how long you expect the exercise to last and tell them what time it is now. Often participants don't look at their watches and therefore have no way of knowing how much time has passed. For example, you have ten minutes for this exercise and it is now 9.30am. This means that they can look at their watches and know how much time has passed since they started the exercise.

What happens at the end of the exercise

It is really important that participants know what is going to happen at the end of an icebreaker. That is, what is going to happen to the information they have just shared. To follow the example through, you might say that each person is going to be asked to share with the group two pieces of information about themselves – one area of involvement in training or one potential area of involvement in training, and the main thing they want out of this training session. When it comes to this part of the icebreaker, then specify exactly how much information you want from each person, before the first person begins with their contribution. If someone who is a little long winded begins this session, you can guarantee that everyone else in the group will give you the same amount of information as the first person. So it is quite acceptable to say something such as, we want two pieces of information from each person, no more than a sentence on each. This means if you have given guidelines about how much information you want, then you can stop any participant who talks for too long. If you haven't given any guidelines then it can be very difficult to shut someone up. It can look as if the participant got it wrong by talking for too long, or that you simply didn't want to hear any more from that person. Either way it doesn't make them a happy bunny and your life long friend.

Although using an icebreaker at the beginning of a training session can have a positive effect on the group's processes and makes contributions easier once everyone has had the opportunity to contribute, there may be occasions when you decide not to use an icebreaker. These are situations where the expectations of the group are for a formal training session – that is when there is only going to be input from the trainer, allowing no contribution from the participants. In this case there would be no need to give any expectations that participants will be encouraged to participate.

Another situation might be where everybody attending the course already knows everyone else. It can be that the trainer is the only one who doesn't know the group. In this case an icebreaker to get everyone to introduce themselves would be for the trainer's benefit only. The trainer needs a strategy to get to know who people are and their job roles. For these situations, use badges or name plates for each participant. Do your homework before the course and find out who does what in the organisation Ask for a list of names and job roles, prior to the course day. When you get people to write their names on a piece of card to display in front of them or on a name badge (that is large enough for you to read) you will be able to put the information together and work out who is who.

In training sessions where all the participants know each other, it is useful to have an exercise at the beginning of the course to get everyone talking to each other, but not necessarily an icebreaker.

Image

When we stand up in front of a group to begin a training session, all eyes are on us. At least – we hope everyone is looking at us, as we need to command the group's attention. Whilst all eyes are on us, participants will be noticing our image. Even if participants are not looking at what we are wearing, in detail, they will notice the overall image we are putting across.

We need to pay attention to what we are wearing. It is said that we have just three minutes to make a good impression. So hopefully the positive way we begin the session is going to help participants to decide that we are a good trainer. To help this we need to think about what we are wearing, what image it gives out, in relation to the group with which we are working.

A trainer needs to choose what to wear carefully, taking into account the group they are working with on that particular day. The idea is not to 'dress to impress', but to dress 'not to be memorable'. That is you want what you said and did and what the participants learnt to be memorable rather than what you wore. The last thing you want participants to say after a training course, is, 'oh yes, I went on that course last week, no I can't remember the trainer's name – it was the one that wears those really short skirts/creased shirts. Yes the course was okay'.

Try and dress in a fairly neutral manner. Nothing too

outstanding or highly fashionable. Wear something that will make you fit in with the group. If you are working with a group of senior managers who you know will arrive in suits, then wear a suit. If you know the group you will be working with will be dressed informally, then do the same. But be neat and tidy. If you don't know the group's dress code, then find out. There is nothing worse than arriving in casual clothes and facing a be-suited set of participants, or vice versa.

If you manage to fit in with the organisation's dress code then you will have a much easier time by being accepted more readily by the group as someone who knows what they are talking about. This will make your life easier. Life can be hard enough, standing up in front of a different group of participants almost every day, without making it harder for yourself with something that is totally within your control.

The other thing to think about, when putting together your training wardrobe, besides versatility (if you work with a wide variety of different groups, then you need the same variety of clothes) is comfort. Believe me, you have enough to think about when you are training, not to need the hassle and distraction of uncomfortable clothes. You need to be able to get dressed in the morning, forget what you are wearing and arrive back home in the evening, looking just as good as when you left. That means, nothing that creases too much, nothing too short (for women) too tight (for men and women), too hot, so that you look like a sweaty heap by lunchtime. In short, nothing you have to think about.

If you develop a wardrobe with clothes you don't have to think about, then you are free to worry about all the other balls that are in the air when you are training!

5
Icebreakers

... an essential ingredient of a trainer's toolbag

An icebreaker is an exercise designed to relax participants at the start of a training course, to get them acquainted with each other, to set the scene for the training and to get them involved, right from the beginning. Icebreaker exercises are very important, as they set the tone for the training.

There are many, many icebreaker exercises that can be used at the beginning of a training course. However an icebreaker needs to be carefully thought through to ensure that it will be the most suitable for both the training content and for the participants. As this will be the first exercise that you ask participants to undertake, then it can set the scene for the rest of the training session, in either a positive or negative way. A good trainer has a large repertoire of icebreakers, ready to use with different groups in different situations. Most icebreakers can be adapted to suit the needs of different groups and different course contents. Here are several icebreaker exercises that can be adapted to your particular training course needs.

Fears in a hat

This icebreaker can be used for the beginning of any course where participants might have some fears or anxieties about participating in the training session. This icebreaker works best with groups of between 8 – 12 participants. If the group is larger than this, the exercise takes too long.

You need to give participants a small piece of paper, and ask them to (a) complete a sentence that you have written on to the flipchart, and to write it on their piece of paper, for example, 'On this training course I am worried about ... ...' or (b) you can ask them to write down a concern or worry they have about being on the course, without having to complete a sentence that you have given them. It is useful to give participants a few examples of the sort of statements they might write, when you set up the exercises, e.g. I'm worried about leaving the dog at home all day, I was worried about finding the venue, I am worried I might have to talk in front of the group, and so on.

When all the participants have written their statement or completed the required sentence, they are then asked to fold their pieces of paper and place them in a 'hat', which is circulated around the group. The 'hat' can be an actual hat or it could be a plastic folder, anything that will be able to be easily passed around the group to collect the pieces of paper. The 'hat' is then shaken and re-circulated around the group, until everyone has read out a 'fear'. After this, if it is appropriate, the group can discuss and perhaps 'own up' to the 'fears' that they have written on the pieces of paper, or the 'fears' can remain anonymous.

This icebreaker is a really good way of getting participants to open up about what might be concerning them. They are usually surprised but reassured when other participants have the same anxieties as they have about attending the training course. Be aware though that you may have some quite timid people on the course and a first exercise that allows people to voice a wide range of 'fears' may reinforce in their minds the possibility of the whole exercise being quite alarming.

True or false

This icebreaker can be used for any size of training event. It is particularly useful on communications skills courses or at the beginning of equality training. But it can be used as a fun starter for any course.

This icebreaker can be used with groups of any size, but would need to be larger than 6 as it would get a bit personal with a very small group. However it can work well with a large group; that is where you are working with over 20 participants.

To set up this icebreaker, you need to divide the group into pairs and have them sitting next to each other, in their own space in the room. Ask each participant to think of three statements about themselves. However, one of these statements should be false and the other two should be true. Working in their pairs, one partner tells the other the three statements. The partner then has to decide which statements are true and which one is false. They then swap the roles and repeat the process. When the exercise has finished, ask participants why they thought a certain statement was false and why they thought that statement were true. You will be asking them to think about what clues, assumptions, and/or prior knowledge were they using, when they were doing the exercise.

When you are setting up this exercise, it is best to tell participants not to make any personal statements that they do not wish the group to know about, as in the discussion following the icebreaker some of the information may be shared. Also when you are setting up the exercise, give the group examples of the sort of statements they might make, depending on the composition of the group, their interests and abilities.

All about me

This icebreaker can be used at the beginning of most training courses when you have half an hour available to run the exercise. On short courses, this exercise takes too long. It is best run with between 8 and 16 participants and therefore is suitable for most training courses, if you have enough time.

You need to give each person a sheet of A3 sized paper, folded into four quarters. Ask them to write their names in the middle of the sheet of paper, where the two creases intersect, and in each of the four corners to write the following:

- their occupation
- a significant person in their life (other than members of immediate family)
- a significant event in their life
- their reason for being here or what they want out of the course.

You should tell them that the information will be shared with the rest of the group, so anything too personal, which they would not wish to share, should be omitted.

Another way to run this exercise is to get participants to 'draw' the information in each box. They can do this by drawing both diagrams and pictures. When the participants move into pairs, then the partner has to guess what the drawing or diagram in each square is representing. This is a much more fun way of running this exercise. However, some groups will need persuading that they have got the abilities to undertake the drawing part of the exercise.

Whether you run the exercise with words or pictures, you then split the group into pairs. Each pair should spend 15 minutes sharing with each other, what they have written on their sheets of paper or guessing what the pictures are about. If you wish, you can extend this exercise by asking each pair to introduce their partners to the rest of the group, but this can take up considerable time.

Sweets

This icebreaker can be used as a fun start to training courses on a wide variety of subjects. It works well on communication and negotiation skills courses. To begin the exercise, give a small bag of 5 sweets of assorted colours to each participant. It is better if you can provide wrapped sweets, as they are going to be handled before they are eaten. Ask them not to eat any of the sweets at this moment. They can do that later. Then explain the object of the exercise to them. This is to get 5 of the same colour sweets in their bag. They should decide which colour sweet is their favourite. The participants may only trade one sweet with another person at one time. This therefore involves the participants circulating around the group, talking to the rest of the participants in an attempt to get a bag of the same colour sweets.

This icebreaker should be run as a light-hearted getting-to-know-you exercise. You need to keep a careful watch on how well participants are doing in getting their bag of the same coloured sweets and call it to a halt after a while. You can check who has got the most of the same coloured sweets. It takes quite a lot of communication between participants to trade the sweets. As you can see, it really is best to choose wrapped sweets as each sweet may have to be handled a few times before the participant is going to eat them.

Newspapers, or not

This icebreaker works best with groups of younger people who enjoy making a mess. Or it can be used as a beginning of an in-house training course when participants don't need any introductions to each other but a warm-up activity is required prior to the start of the training.

The exercise works best with larger groups of maybe 12 and over, as two teams are required and you need to be able to get a bit of 'buzz' into the room. To begin this icebreaker, you need to divide the large group into two 'teams' and separate the room into two halves or sides. You will probably have to improvise on what you use to divide the room (a line of chairs is usually the quickest). Both teams are supplied with a stack of newspapers. When a signal is given each team begins to crumple them up and toss them over the other side (the other team should then toss it back). When you stop the exercise, the team with the least paper on their side wins.

This is a really fun exercise to run, in which most people will become engaged and take part. You will need to explain to the groups before you start the icebreaker that it is meant to be fun and get some energy flowing in the room, or they might wonder why they are being asked to do it. This icebreaker also works well as a warm up session, straight after lunch to liven participants up.

Getting to the nuts and bolts of things

This icebreaker will work with most groups and is useful at times when you want participants to begin to communicate and negotiate with each other early on in the course. This exercise can be used with any group size of more than 8 participants. However it works best with large groups.

Each person is given a nut and a bolt, (that don't fit together). Depending on how long you want the exercise to run you can give each participant a number of miss-matched nuts and bolts.

Participants are then told to move around the training room talking to other participants to try to find the nut or bolt that fits onto theirs. When they have a completed set or sets, they should sit down. This is a really simple exercise which promotes a good deal of discussion and laughter, with people getting nuts stuck on the wrong bolt which usually causes more fun and discussion.

Paper Aeroplanes

This exercise works well with most groups and subject areas, as the information that you will be asking participants to write on to the aeroplane can be varied to reflect the content of the course. This icebreaker is more fun with larger groups of 12 or more participants. To begin the exercise, give everyone a piece of A4 paper. Then demonstrate one way of making a paper aeroplane, in case there are people present who really can't remember how to make one. Then ask people to make a paper aeroplane, either in the way you have demonstrated, or their own preferred method. When the aeroplane is finished the participants should write their name on the plane, and the information you have asked for that is relevant to the course content, for example, what they want to get from the course – or it can be personal information for example, their favourite meal, pop star, country to visit and so on. Once this is complete then the aeroplanes should be launched. Each participant is then invited to pick up someone else's aeroplane and find that person. When they have met up they should help the other to find the owner of their aeroplane. Once you have participants in small groups, they should then share the information that they have written on to the paper aeroplanes.

You need to make sure that the aeroplanes are thrown into the middle of the room, far enough from each participant so that it isn't too obvious which plane belongs to which participant. You will also need to help out to keep the activity moving when participants are trying to find the owners of the aeroplanes.

What's my name?

This is a good icebreaker when you want to start a training course with some noise and a bit of fun. It works best with large groups of 18 plus participants.

First of all ask everyone to stand up. This activity consists of each person approaching another person in the group. They should shake hands with them (if it is appropriate), say hello and give their name. After the introductions, each participant takes the name of their partner as their own.

The introductions continue by moving around the room and repeating the process. At each new introduction, each person takes on the name of the person who has just introduced him or herself to them. The participants should sit down when one of two things happen – they either get their own name back or when you ask everyone to stop and sit down.

You will find that getting participants to take other people's names can make participants feel quite close to each other and can make the group bond together more quickly, and that surprisingly it is a lot of fun and non-threatening.

Numbered groups

This icebreaker is for large groups only (between 20 – 50 participants). It serves the purpose of getting people into small groups in a fun and active way. The outcome of the exercise is that the participants will be divided into small groups. They can then introduce themselves to their group. To start the exercise ask each person in the room to think of a number between 1 – 5 or 1 – 10 depending how many people you have on the course. Then ask them to call out their number quickly, one after another going around the whole group. Next, ask everyone to find the other people with the same number and form a group. They should then introduce themselves to each other.

In the extremely unlikely event of only one person in the whole group choosing a certain number, be vigilant and ask him or her to choose the next number and to join that group.

Getting to know you

This icebreaker is good when you have got plenty of time, about 20 minutes to run this exercise. It makes a good start to longer courses when the group will be spending a considerable amount of time together. It works best with up to a maximum of 10 participants.

To begin the exercise, give each person a piece of A4 paper and ask them to write down three things about themselves, that they don't mind sharing with the rest of the group. You can either tell the group the three things that you want them to write about, for example, their favourite food, TV programme, hobby or lifelong ambition or you can ask them to write three things about themselves of their own choice. Each person should then sign the piece of paper before you collect them in. You should put the pile of papers on the floor in the middle of the group, take a sheet at random and read out the three things (not the name) to the group. The group is then to guess who they think the sheet belongs to and why they think that it belongs to that person.

When you are running this exercise, you need to make sure the group are very clear from the onset that the information is to be shared with the entire group. It is also necessary to keep the guessing upbeat and moving or with a quiet group the exercise can become a bit slow and tedious.

An interesting variant to this theme is to ask the participants to include in the three facts something that no one else in the room could possibly know about them. Often in organisations, people do know a great deal about colleagues and this is an opportunity to add a subtle dimension to the exercise. Things written could be, for example, that the individual was born in South America, collects rare old banknotes or once sang in a choir at a national festival. You can then mentally make a note of these facts (or jot them down) and use the idea later in the course to get that individual to talk about the unusual fact.

6
Setting Up and Running Exercises

... the nuts and bolts of a training session

A good training course usually consists of a mixture of:

- input from the trainer
- group exercises to enable participants to discuss and experience the learning on the course
- discussion facilitated by the trainer.

An effective trainer needs to be skilled at speaking to the group and at running facilitation sessions and also at setting up and running exercises. The latter can often be seen to be the 'easy bit' of running a training session; getting participants into small groups and giving them a task to do should be a piece of cake!

Unfortunately it is sometimes not as easy as it seems. If you watch a skilled trainer performing, setting up exercises looks as if anyone can do it, with very little effort or thought. It all seems to flow, participants understand exactly what they are supposed to be doing, they move to where they should be doing it and the feedback after the exercise is always of good quality.

However, the reality of setting up and running exercises can be very different. Participants need to feel comfortable and that the trainer is in control. Setting up exercises if you are not completely clear and precise with your instructions can be the first crack in any confidence that participants have in your ability as a trainer.

Occasionally, when setting up exercises, you can create a fragile situation something like the proverbial house of cards. One participant who wasn't quite sure about your instructions, either because of your instructions weren't clear, or because he nodded off to sleep when you were giving them, then asks a question about what you want the group to do in the exercise. This usually sets off a chain reaction and other participants start to ask questions about the exercise. Some of them to check what they have missed – perhaps you really didn't explain your instructions well enough – or they were napping, and others join in because they like asking questions.

Whatever the reasons for participants feeling the need to ask the questions, when they start to do it, it can feel like a house of cards that is slowly collapsing around your ears. It can also feel to the participants that you are losing control. Something every trainer wants to avoid at all costs, especially if you are really feeling a little unsure of what you are doing in the first place.

Using exercises on training courses divides into four stages;

- the initial preparation for the exercise
- setting it up with the group
- running the exercise
- taking feedback from the exercise, in order to help participants learn from the activity they have just undertaken.

Each stage is important if participants are really going to learn what you intended them to learn from taking part in the exercise.

Preparation

Before you get in front of the participants with whom you will be working, you need to have thought through the exercises that you want to use on the course, in detail. If you have run the exercises before, you will be aware of any pitfalls or potential areas of difficulty of these particular exercises. If it is the first time that you are going to run them, then you need to think through each step, and list down any points to which you either need to pay special attention or things you specifically need to remember.

The main thing you need to clarify in your own mind it what you want participants to learn from the exercise and how this fits in with the learning outcomes that have been written for the course. If your thinking is woolly at this point when you are deciding how to run the exercises, then it is almost guaranteed that you will be woolly when you start to set them up with a group of participants. Then they won't be clear about exactly you want them to do during each exercise.

The room

Firstly, think about the room layout. Then ask yourself the following questions.

- Is the room big enough to allow participants to have the space to work comfortably on this exercise?
- Would the exercise be better run with participants sitting around tables or perhaps in easy chairs?
- Will there be tables available?
- Will there be easy chairs available?

Some exercises that involve handling or sorting written items, maybe cards, need a table to enable the participants who are working on the exercise to be able to lay out the pieces of the exercise so that everyone can easily see them all. Some exercises that require in-depth discussion are best run with participants being able to sit in comfortable chairs. Being comfortable can make them more willing to discuss in more depth.

- Will participants need to be working in different rooms, so that they cannot hear or see what the other group is doing or talking about?

There are some exercises where is doesn't matter if small groups are working in the same room, others where it is absolutely necessary that they are all working in the same room. Sometimes you don't want them in the same room as you – for instance, when the learning comes from sorting out how to do part of the exercise and you don't want to be available to answer any questions. Putting each small group in a separate room – and separate from you – is usually the best way to run this type of exercise.

The time available

You also need to think about how long the exercise will take the groups to complete. Not only the actual timing of the content, but also how long it will take to get into small groups and to the room in which they are to be working, (if you have allocated them separate rooms). If these rooms are any further away than next door to the main training room, you need to allow an extra 10 minutes for them getting to their group room and back to the main training room. It is surprising, if not amazing, how long it can take a small group to move what only seems like a few yards. But remember, when they reach the room, they then have to settle in, and often have a chat, before they get round to the task in hand. Then they have to get back again to the main training room when they have finished the exercise. For some participants, this can mean coming back to the training room via the toilet or the coffee jug.

Equipment

Then there is the equipment to think about. What equipment will the participants require for the exercise? You need to have it all ready before you introduce the exercise. If you are intending to send the groups off to work in group rooms then it can be useful to put everything they will need into these rooms, before you begin to set up the exercise. Even if all that will be required are sheets of flipchart paper and pens, then have this ready torn off the flipchart pad and make sure you have checked that all the marker pens you are intending the groups to use are working.

If there is quite a lot of equipment needed for the exercise, maybe different sheets or sets of cards, pens, pencils or equipment for team building exercises, then it is best to sort them out and put them into plastic pockets or plastic boxes, one for each group. If the groups are going to be working on different exercises then each 'set' of equipment should be marked. It can all look the same when you are in a hurry to give it out to the groups and get them started on the exercise.

Working together

Then there are the decisions to be made about who will work with whom, during the exercises, and how you will split the large group into the smaller groups that are required to do the exercise. Dividing the large group into smaller groups can be achieved by simply counting around the large group. You can start at one end and count off the first four (if you want four participants in each small group). That is certainly not rocket science, but it will give you a group of four participants all of whom have been sitting near each other. This often means that they know each other, as participants usually sit with people they know when they arrive at a training course.

If you want to separate participants from those they have

been sitting next to, the quickest way to do this is to count round the group in the same way, but with a different outcome. If you have 20 participants in the room and you want them to work in five groups with four people in each, then you count round the group, up to and including the number of groups you want the participants to divide into. So for five groups of four people you would count 1, 2, 3, 4, 5, around the group, asking people to remember the number you have given to them (endeavour not to point at each participant as you go round the group). When you have given everybody a number then you ask all the 1s to work together, all the 2s and so on. This quickly breaks the group into smaller groups, and not working with the people that they were sitting next to in the large group.

This method works in a random way, but you may feel the need to construct the groups who will be working together in a specific way. Maybe you have a few difficult participants whom you feel it would be better for themselves and others, (including you), if they didn't work together. Or maybe the reverse could be true; that you feel it would be beneficial if they did work together at this particular point on the course. Maybe you have both managers and staff in the group and you want to make sure that you have a mixture of both in all the groups, because this would be better learning experience for them all.

To do this, find a way of dividing the large group so, that if you are challenged by a participant as to why certain people were in certain groups, you will be able to give them a reason, other than, in some cases, the truth. Of course, it is okay to tell participants that you wanted a mix of staff and managers working together, but it is not quite so easy to tell some participants that you thought that they were being difficult and you didn't want them working in certain groups with certain people. This sort of information is usually best kept to yourself, as there is absolutely no point in digging a hole for yourself, over this issue.

So, you need to work out a formula for how to divide groups into smaller groups. One way to do this is to use the participant list that you will no doubt have been supplied with at the beginning of the course. For example, you can take the first two participants on the list, and then miss two names, and put the next two names with the first two names to make a group of four.

Whatever method you decide to use in order to form the groups that you think will work best together, remember what you did and then if you are asked you will have a ready answer. If you are challenged as to why certain groups were formed, it is usually by the 'difficult' participants who don't want to work in the group that you had put them in, don't want to be on the training course, or are looking for something to pick about. There is even more need to have not only a ready but a plausible answer in situations like these. Participants really don't like to be patronised or see the trainer seemingly playing god and moving them around like pawns on a chessboard, or behaving like the teacher they still hate, from their school days, who moved them to different seats around the classroom, on what seemed merely a whim.

Setting up an exercise

When you have done all your preparation for an exercise, the setting up will be much simpler. This is because you are absolutely clear in your own mind what you want participants to do, why you want them to do it, how you want them to do it, and what they will learn as a result of doing it.

- When you are setting up an exercise, first **introduce the subject** area and give participants any background information that they need to make sense of the exercise.

- **Explain the exercise**, giving clear instructions of how they are going to carry it out.

- Write the **key points and/or instructions** onto a flipchart, unless you have pre-prepared printed sheets for each group to use which will be given to them at the appropriate time in the setting up of the exercise. Writing down the instructions either on sheets of paper or onto the flipchart gives participants an opportunity to check back during the exercise to make sure that they are still on track.

- Tell participants how you want them to either divide into small **groups**, or how you are going to divide them. Tell them the method that will be used, but also tell them that it is going to happen in a minute or two. You want to keep everyone seated and paying attention to what you are saying until you have finished giving them all the instructions that they will need to carry out the exercise.

- Tell participants how they are going to **record** their discussion or **findings** from the exercise. There are various alternatives, but usually groups are requested to record any discussion or findings onto a piece of A4 paper or a flipchart sheet, or onto post-it notes or on pieces of card. It all depends on what you want the groups to do with the information at the end of the exercise.

- Ask them to elect a person from the group to act as the **scribe** for the duration of the exercise and to explain what you will be looking for as feedback from the exercise and how this feedback will be given by the group, after the exercise.

- Ask them to elect the person who is going to give the **feedback** to the larger group, on behalf of the rest of the group members. This gives the group the opportunity to organise themselves ready for the end of the exercise, rather than having to do it when you call time, and therefore holding up the process of the training.

- Next, tell participants **how long** they have got to carry out the exercise. Then tell them what the time is now. There is little point in telling groups that they have 20 minutes without them knowing when the 20 minutes actually began. Very few participants actually look at their watches when they are busy starting and carrying out an exercise.

- Ask the group to elect a **timekeeper**, to try and get over the problem of none of the group members looking at their watches.

- Then when you have done all this, **run through the whole thing again**! Point out the instructions you have written up on the flipchart. (If participants are working in separate rooms it is useful to have them written up on flipchart sheets in each room). Remind participants of the objectives of the exercise and the method that they will be using to reach these objectives, and the timing.

- Now give out any **paperwork** that is necessary for them to carry out the exercise.

- Finally get them to **move into the groups** that you require for the exercise. Then tell them what the time is now and how long they have got from this point, and what the time will be when it's finished. For example, it is now 10 o'clock – the exercise will last for 30 minutes, which means you need to be finished by 10.30am. It seems to be all very pedantic but you truly need to work in this amount of detail to ensure participants know exactly what they should be doing and very importantly, why they are doing it.

Running the exercise

The third stage, after the preparation and the setting up of the exercise, is running the exercise. Participants should now all be hard at work in their small groups, in their allocated areas of the training room, or in their small group room. Your job is now to check that they have really understood what they are supposed to be doing and are getting on with it.

At this stage, don't go up into the groups and interfere with what they are doing. Even the question, 'how are you getting on?' can interrupt with the group process. This sort of interruption from the trainer usually results in them stopping and telling you what they have done so far. This can then put them back on completing the exercise and one of the keys to running successful exercises is getting all groups to finish at the same time. There is almost nothing worst than some of the groups having finished their exercise, sitting twiddling their thumbs waiting for another group to finish. It can be very demotivating for the other participants. Often in these situations, conversation turns to last night's television or the latest football match and participants are beginning to lose interest in what ever they have discovered by doing the exercise.

When running exercises, it is best to stroll around the training room, stick your head into the small rooms and smile at the participants. If they really do have any problems then they will ask you. Listen to the groups working, check out that their discussion sounds as if it is on track. Observe the body language of the participants to try and get a clue as to what is happening in the small groups. You should be able to take an educated guess as to whether things are going well or not.

If you are happy that all the groups are on track, sit back and let them get on with it. This can be your time to collect your thoughts and prepare for the next part of the training course. But at the same time keep your eye on what is happening in the small groups, keep observing participants' body language and keep listening in to the groups to have a 'feel' for what is happening. Only get involved with a group if you feel things are going off track. Your main role during the running of the exercise is to act as a timekeeper.

Tell the groups, at intervals, how much longer they have got before they need to have the exercise completed. It is useful to do this, even if you have asked the groups to elect their own timekeepers. The individual participant who has been elected as timekeeper will often forget if they are really involved in the exercise.

When running exercises on a training course, one of the difficulties can be ensuring that all the groups finish at the same time. If a group finishes early, then you need to acknowledge that they have finished early and find something for them to do whilst they are waiting for the other groups to finish. This needs to be appropriate to the exercise and not look as if you are treating them like children who have to have something to do to keep them out of mischief. Maybe you can ask them to prioritise their findings or discuss a particular point in more detail, that can then be picked up at the feedback session.

The minimum you can do is to acknowledge that they have finished earlier than the other groups and ask them to wait until the other groups have finished. You need to discourage them from going to get an extra cup of coffee or having a wander around. It is much better to keep them seated and in their group, as having them moving around can be disruptive for the other groups who are still working.

Conversely, if a group seems to be taking a long time to do the exercise, intervene and get them to move on a bit faster.

Maybe discussion has stuck on a certain point, or maybe they are disagreeing on an issue. Try and resolve the point and move them on. Remember, your goal is to get them all to finish at the same time and within the time that you have allocated for the exercise.

If all the groups have finished earlier than the time you had allocated for the exercise, make a note of this for yourself and see if it happens again the next time you run the same exercise with a different group of participants. If it does, then you know that maybe you got your timings a little wrong. If none of the groups look as if they are going to finish in the time you have allocated, and are taking longer than you expected, you need to concede to the groups' needs for extra time and change your timings.

Let all the groups know that you are extending the time for the exercise, by the amount of time that you think is necessary for them to complete the exercise and not feel rushed or hurried. You then need to look at what you had planned for the rest of the training course and see where you can shave off some minutes, so that you can still finish on time.

Running training courses is all about tucking and stretching the material to fit in with the participants and the timing. That is shortening some of the content either by employing another method to enable you to get the material over in a quicker way, or taking longer on some of the areas on the course if you feel participants want to discuss the area more fully. A training course never runs like clockwork and each training course you run will be different in how the participants respond to the material. Some groups can get involved in a really deep discussion about the topic they are working on, whereas others get the task done in record time, and often covering all the points that is has taken other groups twice as long to come up with.

Taking feedback

The fourth stage of running exercises is taking any feedback that is necessary to the exercise and to the learning. This is getting each group to tell the other groups and yourself what they have discussed or what they have found out, as a result of doing the exercise and what they have learnt from the experience. As the trainer, you have to be clear about what you were expecting from the groups, when you were setting up the exercise, so that all the groups have been clear about what was expected of them at this stage, and the feedback follows a similar pattern from each group.

One of the inherent problems on training courses is what can be the tedious nature of receiving feedback. If each group is telling the other groups about what they have discussed or found out, then as all the groups have been doing the same exercise, their findings may well be the same or similar. Often the only difference is the way it is expressed by whoever is giving the feedback. In fact, you hope the feedback is similar – if it isn't, it means that one of the groups has gone off track from the exercise, and has not covered what you wanted them to cover.

A rule of thumb is, when taking feedback from small groups after an exercise, only use the method where each group tells the other groups about their finding, if you have no more than three small groups. It is just about possible to hear the same thing, said in different words, three times, and still stay a little bit interested. Remember, the small groups have also just had the entire discussion in their groups, which means that they are hearing it four times. One could argue that repetition reinforces learning, but it is probably truer to say that it induces boredom.

So, when you are planning the exercise, think about how many small groups you are going to set up in relation to both the numbers that the exercise will work the best with and how you are going to take any feedback. Try and think of creative ways of taking feedback, for example, sometimes it is possible to set up the exercise, so that each small group can work on different parts of the subject area. Of course, this is not always possible but some subject areas lend themselves to this method.

If you have more than three groups, then you could get each group to display the flipchart sheets where they have recorded their findings, on the training room walls. Then all the groups could circulate around the room and read the information on each other's flipchart sheets.

You could also restrict the feedback from each group, maybe asking for two or three main points from their findings. You would of course have to give them a warning that this was what you were going to ask for, a few minutes before the exercise was due to finish, or if it was appropriate when you were setting up the exercise.

There is the option of not taking feedback from each group on the exercise, but moving straight into a large group discussion on the exercise or even, if it is appropriate, to move on to the next part of the training course. Always remember that the participants have had the discussion once already in their small groups.

How you take feedback at the end of an exercise depends on how you want to move on to the next part of the training course and how important the feedback will be to the participants learning and how it links to the next session.

If you can set up and run exercises smoothly, participants will feel comfortable to learn, as you will be creating a safe atmosphere, where you appear to be in control of what is going on. Remember, one of the ingredients of what makes a good trainer is being in control. This is a skill that is tested when setting up and running exercises.

7
Facilitating Training Exercises

... should you stand up or sit down?

What is the difference between facilitation and training? It is a question that can often be a puzzle to trainers. People who do not know too much about the training process often misuse the two words. You can be asked to facilitate a workshop at a conference and find that actually what is required is a forty-five minute slot of input on a particular subject with some time for questions at the end. This is hardly facilitation.

What is usually meant is a session within a training course where the participants have an opportunity to explore their thoughts, ideas and knowledge around a particular subject. Or it could be the whole of a session where you as the trainer have been brought in to get the group to explore certain issues. In these cases, it is often about areas such as which way the organisation needs to move forward or how the staff group either work or don't work as a team and how things could be improved, allowing the staff group to come up with the reasons and ideas themselves as opposed to being told what they should do to improve the situation.

Trainers often think this type of work is easier than actual training, where you have to 'teach' the group a concept or idea. In actual fact, running a facilitation can demand a higher level of skills and ability from the trainer. To be a good facilitator, you need to be a skilled questioner, and an excellent listener. You need to be able to stay impartial and objective and you need to be able to move the group on when they get stuck. You also need to be skilful at leading from behind, rather than from the front.

Leading from behind, that is nudging the group forward, without them feeling you are in anyway directing or being in control can be very stressful for the trainer, especially when you think you can see an easier way forward than the tortuous route the group seemed to have chosen. Some trainers are more comfortable to act as facilitators than other trainers. Listening and enabling the group to move forward can come more naturally to some trainers. Other trainers are happier and feel more comfortable standing at the front of the training room directing the group. The latter can often feel safer, to a trainer, because at least you think you know what is going to happen and in what order it is going happen – although things don't always go to plan in all training situations.

However, it is a myth that a facilitation just happens; that the trainer throws out a question and the group picks it up and from there on there is a deep and interesting discussion about the subject in hand. Some groups will talk about anything and discuss the subject in depth. Others will sit in near silence with the odd contribution coming from just one or two individual members of the group. If you are lucky enough to have the first group, then your life, for that amount of time, will be easier. However, as those types of groups are thin on the ground, then it is advisable to prepare for a facilitation.

You have to decide what needs to be covered within the subject area. You cannot plan for how the group will get there, but you need to have the content mapped out, so at the end of the facilitation there isn't an important chunk of the subject that has been missed out of the discussion. This applies whether you are running a whole day's facilitation with a group or are using it as a method to break up the training into interesting chunks.

Planning for a facilitation exercise

To run an effective facilitation exercise, the planning needs to be very thorough. The first thing to decide when you are planning for a facilitation is what is the subject that you are going to get the group to discuss. Not a vague idea of what it is, but referring back to the objectives for the training and taking it from there. Ask yourself – what do participants need to learn from this session? What is the outcome for it? Once you have decided what is going to be under discussion, then you can build up the content that the participants need to cover in the session.

The next step in the planning is to take a blank piece of paper, and write the subject area that you are going to cover, in the middle of the page. Then start to develop a spider diagram around this subject area. Each 'leg' of the spider diagram will cover an area, within the main subject area, that you wish participants to cover in their discussion. Once you have all the areas that need to be discussed on your spider diagram, you should then start to build up more detail around the content of each 'leg'. When you have finished, your piece of paper should be quite detailed, containing everything that you want the group to discuss when you are running the facilitation exercise.

The whole point of doing this is that the trainer needs to have thought out in detail what the group needs to cover in its discussion. You can't leave it to chance and hope that the group will come up will all the ideas. If you have a plan in front of you whilst you are facilitating the session, then you don't have to think on your feet when the group goes quiet and can't think of anything else that needs to be discussed. You have enough things to do when you are thinking of questions to keep the group on track or to challenge them into another level of thinking about the subject: watching the timing; making sure that every one has an opportunity to contribute; bringing quiet people in to the discussion; and ensuring the more talkative participants don't dominate the session.

When you have built up your spider diagram, the next stage is to think about the questions you will ask to get the facilitation going and to keep it on track.

Different types of questions

There are different types of questions, some more useful to a facilitation that others. To be a good facilitator you must be skilful at designing and asking questions.

Open questions
In a facilitation exercise, you should be using more open questions than other types. These are questions that should enable participants to give a lot of information or thoughts to the question, without biasing the response. It should be difficult to answer a good open question with a 'yes' or a 'no' answer. An open question frequently begins with what, why, when, where, who or how. However, if you do begin your question with any of those words, it is possible to get a very short, almost one word answer. For example, *'How did to get to the training course today?'* you ask a participant. You have begun the question with one of the suggested words. The participant, who isn't very talkative, replies by saying, 'by car.' This has not exactly opened up discussion on the various modes of transport open to participants or to the difficulties of getting to the venue.

One thing to be remembered is that usually the quality of the response to a question is in direct correlation to the quality of the question that has been posed. The onus is on you, as the trainer, or in this case the facilitator to come up with quality questions, to ensure the exercise is worth taking part in, for everybody.

A better way to begin an open question is to preface the who, what, why, when, where or how with a short phrase, such as, tell me about… or describe to me… So, you could ask the same question again, by saying, *'Tell me about your journey to the training session today.'* This gives the participant the idea that you want to know more than just what method of transport he or she used.

Closed questions

Closed questions are those that can be answered with a single word, for example, *'Do you think this is a good idea?'* Closed questions can be used to obtain precise facts, or to slow up a talkative person and are unlikely to bias the response. However in a facilitation exercise, closed questions should be kept to a minimum and only used when you need a participant to give you a precise fact, perhaps to back up something else they have said, or to clarify something they or someone else has contributed to the discussion. Closed questions can discourage quiet people from participating and can be perceived by the group as an interrogation. Unfortunately, closed questions are always the easiest to think of, especially when you are under pressure. A facilitation exercise can easily turn into a question and answer session if the facilitator falls into this trap.

Leading questions

This is a question which indicates the response in the question, for example, *'Presumably you feel like that because …'* A leading question is likely to influence the participant answering it into making the desired response and therefore should not be used when you are facilitating. The group will begin to think that you have an agenda that you are trying to get them to work on, when in fact you just have poor questioning skills. This will either provoke the group into disagreeing with you wholesale about the subject under discussion, and becoming difficult or, if the subject is not that close to their hearts, losing interest and giving up making any attempts to join in with the discussion. Either way, a difficult situation for the trainer to put right.

Limiting questions

This is a question which narrows down the field of response open to the participants. For example, *'Do you prefer this idea or that idea?'* It is acceptable to use this type of question towards the end of the facilitation exercise, when a lot of the views about the subject under discussion have been aired. It gives you an opportunity to get the group to begin to narrow down a range of ideas that have been expressed during the discussion.

Comparative questions

This is a question that seeks to establish preferences, priorities or rankings and can be used to get participants to sort out responses into a preferred order. For example, *' We have discussed options in regard to how a customer service package could be implemented in this organisation – how would you rate them in order of importance?'* Again, these questions can be useful towards the end of a facilitation exercise when the issues have been discussed and you might want to draw together all the threads.

Multiple questions

Multiple questions are questions that have several components to them. For example, *'What do you think about the organisations customer service policy, how do you think it should be implemented and who should do it?'* These types of questions are usually unplanned and frequently cause confusion to the participants because they don't know which part of the question to answer first. Obviously this is a question type to avoid when you are running a facilitation exercise. It will not get discussion going, but will more often be met by the group with a stunned silence.

Super questions
These questions are questions that contain words like, specifically, precisely, exactly. For example, *'Describe to me exactly what you did to implement x system?'* These questions signal to the participants that you want detailed information from them. Most of us answer questions with generalities, usually concerned that we might bore people if we go into detail. (There is always the exception to this!) By using super questions, you can get the group to discuss the subject in more detail.

Developing questions in the planning stage

The next step in the planning for a facilitation exercise is to think about what questions you are going to ask. The first question you need to think about is the opening question for the facilitation. This has got to be good. It needs to be an open question. It needs to be addressed to the whole group. This question will hopefully arouse the interest and curiosity of the participants and focus the attention of the group. It needs to be broad enough in its scope to encompass the subject that is going to be under discussion, but tight enough to enable participants to have a clue as to how to answer it. If have you ever been asked that awful interview question, *'Tell me about yourself'*, then you will appreciate how difficult it is to know where to start with open questions that are so broad. A better question would be, *'Tell me about what you have done in your working life that relates to the job for which you have applied?'* This gives the interview candidate a few hooks to start with when they are gathering their answer together in their heads.

The same applies to a facilitation exercise. The first question needs to be broad enough to have plenty of scope for answering, but not too broad that no one knows where to start with an answer (that way, you get that awful silence you are usually trying to avoid). So think about it carefully. Get this right and you are on your way to facilitating a good session.

Once you have decided on the opening question then you can start working on the other questions that you might use during the facilitation exercise. Look at each leg of the spider diagram and devise one or two questions that would give you the information you are looking for in that area. Then go further down the leg of the spider diagram and think of 'smaller' open question, or limiting or comparative questions you might use later on in the discussion. Write these on your spider diagram in the appropriate place. There is only a 'might' use them at this stage because you don't know how the discussion is going to pan out in real life. You may not need the questions if discussion is flowing. But it makes you feel more confident if they are there ready for you to use. This will help you to avoid falling into the trap of using too many closed questions and turning the exercise into an interrogation.

Preparing your notes

Now you have your spider diagram and your questions ready prepared. But before you run the facilitation exercise, it is useful to refine your preparation a little more. You have put down everything you feel should be covered in the discussion. Now have a look at it again and prioritise areas that must be discussed and others that can be discussed if there is enough time or could be left out if time runs out. You can colour code these so you can see at a glance which areas are important

Write your questions in another colour to make sure that these are easy to spot when you need them. Make sure you can read your spider diagram easily, that is it is large enough to see without having to look at it closely because you will be using this as your 'notes' when you run the facilitation exercise.

Running a facilitation exercise

Now all the preparation has been done, the whole process has been well thought out and questions prepared, running a facilitation exercise becomes a much easier and a less daunting task for a trainer. When you are running a facilitation exercise, sit down. It is best to sit slightly to the side of the group. The impression you want to give is that you are not in charge during this discussion; you are only there to nudge it along the right lines. Standing up will stultify the discussion and probably turn the exercise into a question and answer session led by the trainer. Even sitting directly facing the group can give them the feeling that the discussion has to go through the trainer, as if you were chairing the session.

The best compliment a group can give you after you have facilitated the session is that they forgot you were there. Of course you know you are in control, but it doesn't need to appear that way to them. You should start by introducing the subject that is going to be discussed and saying what outcome the group is working towards. This could be as simple as everyone having thought about the subject area or that the group needs to come to a decision about how they are going to proceed with x.

Then start with your main question. This will be what is

called an overhead question, which is addressed to the whole group. Anyone may answer. Its primary function is to stimulate the groups thinking and get discussion goi j. You may get an answer from one person or several may attempt to answer. Whatever the response is to the question will determine which area of the discussion will come under debate first. This is where a spider diagram really becomes much more useful than a set of notes written in a linear fashion. The answer that this particular participant has given should take the discussion on to one of the legs of the spider. If you have thought the whole thing out well enough there should be nothing that a participant says that you haven't thought of already.

Maybe some one will come at something from a slightly different angle, but you still will have thought of the area. So the discussion will stay on that 'leg' of the spider diagram for a while. Then some one may make a contribution that takes the discussion onto another area of the spider diagram. Whilst this is happening, you will be able to chart what the discussion has already covered, and what still needs to be discussed. If you can do it discreetly, then you can tick off the areas as the group has discussed them. Using this spider diagram also means that if discussion gets stuck, you can see which areas need to be covered and you can use one of your pre-prepared questions to move the discussion on to that area.

This method is particularly useful for a facilitation exercise because the discussion can be jumping about all over the place and this means that you have a pictorial view of the discussion, making it much easier to ensure that the group gets to the outcome that was planned.

Handling the group

For a facilitation exercise to feel positive, then all the group must be involved. That usually means the facilitator having to both bring participants into the discussion and shut them out of it.

When trying to involve participants in the discussion, always say their name first before you ask them a question or maybe ask them to comment on what has just been said. This is really important if you don't want participants to feel they are being put on the spot. In particular the shy or reserved participants who don't naturally feel happy when speaking in front of a group.

Do you remember being at school? Say, in a maths lesson, actually only physically being there, mentally you were somewhere much more interesting, perhaps on a beach, with white sand and a clear blue sea. You can hear the murmur of a voice in the distance and then quite clearly, your name. The teacher has asked you a question that you didn't hear and now is waiting for you to reply. You clutch at straws and say 49 (just in case by any chance the question had been 7x7). You know that actually you had more chance of winning the lottery than that being the question you had been asked. Do you remember the feeling of your stomach turning over and everyone looking at you? Teachers use this as a method of control to embarrass pupils into not daydreaming. As trainers working with adults, you want to avoid evoking any bad memories of learning. So you must always say the participant's name first, give him or her the opportunity to come back from the imaginary beach they were sitting on.

Then you ask the question, or repeat what some one has just said that you were asking them to comment on. This way they don't feel put on the spot and are more likely to continue to be involved in the process. Every one of us has that few seconds when we switch off from what is being said. On a training course, it's not about catching the participants doing it, but developing a positive learning climate so that they don't want to be momentarily or longer, mentally somewhere else. (Mind you, if the individual *is* sitting on an imaginary beach, this means that your efforts to run a totally absorbing and meaningful training session are beginning to fail – at least for one participant. Watch out!)

Shutting people up can be more difficult. But everyone needs to be given an equal opportunity to contribute. When you feel someone is dominating the discussion too much, you need to ask them to be quiet for a while to give some one else a chance to speak. Again you don't want to alienate them either from the process or from the group. Whatever you say to them, you need to ensure that your body language follows what you are saying. If you say something like, 'that was very interesting, let's see what others think about it', and continue to look at that person, nodding and smiling then they will probably continue to talk and tell you more. This is because they are reading your body language which conveys 55% of the message, your tone of voice which is encouraging and conveys 38% of the message and the words which you are saying, which are really, shut up, that's enough, but are only conveying 7% of the message. So it's hardly surprising that they carry on talking.

What you must do is use body language that tells them it is time for some one else to make a contribution. The best way to do this is to break eye contact with them and turn to someone else the second you have finished saying that their contribution was interesting. The bit about 'let's hear from some one else' is directed either at an individual, or at a different section of the group. Trainers often blame the individual for not being able to shut up when actually it is they that are sending out mixed messages.

8
Starting and Controlling Discussions

... some tricks of the trade

The dictionary defines discussion as 'the exchange of opinions, debate or argument'. In training terms, this covers a multitude of things. It can be a structured discussion lead by the trainer, with a specific aim in mind, as covered in the previous chapter on facilitation. Similarly, it can be a free discussion where the group has most of the control over the direction taken, but with the trainer making sure that all the necessary points are covered by the group.

The way the discussion is run will depend, in part at least, on the nature of the subject and type of course in which it occurs. But it also depends on the group with which you are working. Some groups need help to ensure that everyone gets a chance to participate, bringing some participants into the discussion and sometimes making sure some participants don't dominate the session. It is often useful to use different discussion techniques to vary the methods on your training courses. Some subjects work best when there is some structure planned into the discussion.

Getting a discussion going and controlling it to achieve the objectives of the training can be a tricky business. The discussion techniques in this chapter will give you extra ideas for ways of both developing and controlling discussions.

Being able to think on your feet is an important skill for any trainer. The more ideas that you have for different ways of doing things on training courses, the more confident you will feel, and the more skilled you will appear.

Each discussion technique in this chapter has clear instructions to enable you to integrate them into your training courses. Some techniques you will want to plan into your courses, others you can use if things are not working out as you had hoped. Either way, you will find the techniques in this chapter an invaluable addition to your 'trainer's tool bag'.

When running a discussion exercise, you should try to remain neutral during the discussions. It is your role to start off the discussion and to encourage as wide a participation as possible from the group, usually by using questions or different techniques to keep the discussion on the desired subject.

Preparing for a discussion

Some discussions can arise spontaneously during a training session with no preparation by the trainer. For example, a participant may make a statement with which another participant disagrees. The trainer can allow the discussion to develop by bringing in the rest of the group. Other discussion will be the result of the trainer deliberately starting the ball rolling.

When preparing for a discussion, the trainer will need to consider what learning outcomes are to be achieved by the discussion. You can use the discussion technique when the group has knowledge or experiences of the subject and differing opinions are likely to exist. You can also use it at the start of a course or session in order to establish the level of knowledge of the group. In addition, these techniques can be used during or after a session in order to check the participants' understanding, or to improve their understanding and as an aid to the retention of the information. It is also useful where the learning outcomes of the course are to influence attitudes or behaviour in situations where the trainers telling the participants may be construed by the participants as preaching.

Advantages of discussion

When working with adults, it is very usual for them to react badly if their experiences and the expertise that they bring to the training situation are not recognised by the trainer. The participants on a training session are less likely to feel as if they are being 'told' as opposed to being 'asked', if they have been engaged in some discussion about the issue or subject in question. They are more likely to accept the opinions and views of their peers than those of the trainer, at certain times on the training course. In addition high participation by the participants can help them to maintain their interest. When participants are contributing to a discussion, they can be asked to explain or justify what they are saying, which may promote deeper, clearer thoughts on the subject. Also by participating in the discussion it will help them to retain the knowledge.

Disadvantages of discussion

When running a discussion, it can be dominated by one or two strong personalities. If this happens, then you can lose some control over the content of the session. Another problem with discussions is that it can be expensive in terms of the time that it uses up. Also strongly-held differences of opinion can damage any group cohesion that you have worked so hard to build up, which can inhibit learning, especially for the quieter participants in the groups. All of these disadvantages can be alleviated to some extent by the trainer working hard to understand what is happening in the group at any point in time.

Starting a discussion

Once you have identified the learning outcomes for the discussion and the subject area has been chosen, you need to find a way of starting and controlling the discussion. There are various methods that you can use.

To start a discussion, you may decide to make a statement and ask for comments. For example, *'It has been suggested that people only work for the money and the only way to improve their output is to pay them more.'* You may pose a question. For example, *'How do we motivate staff coming to the end of a contract?'*

Once you have started the discussion, you need to control it. With some groups, this is quite easy, but with other groups of participants you may need to impose some structures on the processes to keep the group moving in the right direction. Sometimes it is useful to impose some structures on a discussion because it can make undertaking the exercises more interesting for the participants and vary the course methods.

Here are a variety of suggestions for running and controlling group discussions

Opinion Cards

There are two ways of running this discussion technique, the first method is where the trainer prepares a set of statements about the subject to be discussed and writes each one on a separate piece of card. The statements should be either controversial or open ended, to encourage the participants to discuss them. The set of cards on which the statements have been written are placed in a pile in the middle of the group. In addition, the group has a sheet of flipchart paper on which has been drawn a continuum, with 'disagree' written at one end of the continuum and 'agree' written at the other.

One person begins the discussion by picking up the first card in the pile and reading it out loud, to the rest of the group. That person then makes a decision about his or her relative agreement or disagreement with the statement on the card. He or she places it on the continuum, in a position that reflects relative agreement or disagreement with the statement. The participant then explains to the group why the card was placed it where it is on the continuum.

Once this has been done, the whole group discusses the statement and the issues involved. Once the group has exhausted their discussion on that particular statement, as a group they decide where the card should be placed on the continuum.

The process is continued with different participants starting each new topic, until the group has discussed all the cards and they are all placed on the continuum, displaying the group's relative agreement or disagreement with them.

Another way to run this discussion technique is to give all the participants a blank card and ask them to write a statement about the subject to be discussed on to the cards. This could be a controversial statement that the participants either believe or don't believe, or some aspect of the subject area that they would like to discuss. These are then collected up and the same process is used as before to get discussion going.

The benefits of using this discussion technique is that everyone in the group is given an equal opportunity to both initiate and participate in the discussion. The discussion is more focused, especially if you write the statements on to the cards, as you will be able to initiate the scope of the discussion.

Rounds

The technique is useful when discussion has got 'stuck', or where a decision has to be made by the group, or in situations where some participants have been silent for a long period of time. If you instigate a 'round', it is possible to restart the discussion and bring the silent participants back into the framework.

To run a round you ask each person, in turn, around the training room to respond to the question you have posed or request you have made to the group. For example you could ask, *'What are your views on this now?'* or *'How are you feeling about this now?'* or *'What do you want to do next?'* It is useful to tell participants that they can say 'pass', if they are not ready to make a contribution when it is their turn, and you will go back to them. It is also necessary to tell participants that it is acceptable to repeat what others have already said during the round. Otherwise the participants whose turn comes at the end of the round could spend more time trying to think of something different to say, rather can giving their true feelings or opinions.

Each contribution made by participants should be greeted with silence and you should move straight on to the next person. You don't want the discussion to start again until everybody has had their say about the subject under discussion.

Once everyone has heard what everyone else has to say,

then all the participants and you will have a clear picture of each other's viewpoints. This will often have made participants start to listen to each other again, if discussion had become heated and had deteriorated. It also should have served the purpose of bringing in the quiet people and also bringing in those who may have lost interest in the discussion.

Dilemma Boards

This discussion technique works best when a problem needs to be discussed or needs to be solved by the participants on the training course. The problematic situation is written in the centre of the flipchart. Then four different responses or solutions to that dilemma are written, one in each corner of the same piece of paper. The participants are then invited to come out to the flipchart and put a tick in the square where their preferred option is written.

When everyone has made a choice, the group discusses why each person chose the option they have ticked. At any point in the discussion, participants can change their mind about which is their preferred option and can come out to the front and cross out their tick in the square that they had chosen and put a tick in the square of their new choice.

At the end of the discussion, it might become clear where the groups preferences lay, but it is up to you as the trainer to bring the session to an appropriate close. Another way of working with this technique is to get the participants to come up with the options to put in each of the squares on the flipchart. The best way to do this is to get each participant to write a preferred response on a post-it note. Then you take each note and sort it onto the flipchart into the four or six areas. Disregard any (with the group's agreement) that are a 'one-off'. Put others together which are similar.

The benefits of using this discussion technique is that the first part of the exercise – when participants choose their preferred option or the post it notes are put on the flipchart with their preferred responses written on to them – visually maps out the group's thoughts on the matter to be discussed or resolved. The discussion that follows will be more focussed and structured as the group discusses each option.

Matches

This discussion technique is very useful when you are working with a group where there are some dominant members or excessively quiet people, or if you are unlucky enough to have both types of participants. This technique controls the input of all the participants. Each person is allocated a number of spent matches (up to ten) depending on the number of people in the group and the amount of time available for the exercise. Seven participants with ten matches each is about the right number for a twenty-minute discussion. When participants make a contribution, they put one of their matches into the centre. When they have used all of their matches, they cannot make any further contributions.

This discussion technique highlights who speaks often and who speaks infrequently. It also increases awareness of the length of contribution that individual participants make to the discussion. When the people who speak the most have used up their matches, then those left, who are often the ones who speak the less or who normally find it difficult to break into a discussion are able to continue. This technique is great to use when working with groups who find it difficult to listen to each other or with groups where there are dominant members.

The Beautiful Object

Another discussion technique that is very useful for controlling discussion is 'the beautiful object'. This is similar to the previous technique but, in addition, tends to also slow down discussion, giving participants more time to think about what they want to contribute and more opportunity to listen to other people's contributions.

The beautiful object should be something that is pleasant and easy to hold – it could be a polished stone, an onyx egg, a paperweight, a small ornament or a polished wooden stick. Any person wanting to make a contribution has to be holding the object, before they can speak. The 'object' should be put down on a table, or on the floor in the middle of the group when the person who was holding it has finished their contribution, ready to be picked up by the next person who wants to make a contribution.Possession or holding of the 'object' which is pleasant and easy to hold, entitles any participant to speak and have the attention of the group. Participants must indicate that they want the 'object' before they can make a contribution to the discussion. The 'object' is then passed from person to person within the group. No one may speak unless he or she is holding the 'object', even to make a small contribution or merely interrupt.

The benefit of this discussion technique is that it slows down discussion and ensures that participants listen to each other. The passing of the object is a visible representation of the pattern of the discussion. It also increases the awareness of how often individuals speak and for how long. Sometimes people who find it difficult to break into a discussion find it much easier to hold out their hand for the object and then speak. Additionally the use of holding the 'beautiful object' makes interruptions much more obvious as they are not acceptable within the 'rules' of this exercise.

The disadvantages are that it really does slow down discussion and therefore some participants can get frustrated with the activity. It is therefore best only to keep this technique going for short periods of time. You can always reintroduce it if discussion gets out of hand at any point.

9

Using Visual Aids

... and avoiding the gremlins

Visual aids can be a nightmare for trainers. Any trainer who is nervous at the thought of standing up in front of a group can often feel as if he or she is going to be taken over the edge when faced with having to use visual aids. Visual aids often contain 'gremlins', that no amount of practicing beforehand with the visual aids, will manage to eliminate.

'Gremlins' isn't a technical term in training, but it does describe what happens to some visual aids when you start to use them. It is the leg of the flipchart stand that trips you over almost every time you try and walk past it; it is the video tape that seems to be in the wrong place when you were sure that you had checked it; it is the overhead projector transparencies that were in the right order when you left home, but now you are using them they don't seem to be in sequence, anymore.

The most used visual aids on training courses are flipcharts, videos, overhead projectors and Powerpoint presentations. Each one of them has hidden dangers for the unsuspecting trainer.

So, why use them, if they are such a minefield? Well, participants learn and retain information better if they can see

113

it written down. 75% of information received by the brain, comes through the eyes; 12% comes through the ears. Therefore, using visual aids will help to reinforce the learning of the participants on a training course.

When the trainer uses visual aids it can also make it easier for participants to take notes. The other use of visual aids is as a benefit to the trainer. The visual aid that has been pre-prepared can be used as prompts for the trainer. This means that you can use them as notes. Imagine if you have your four points about what ever it is that you will be talking about, ready printed on the overhead transparency that you are using, then you can talk to the participants from the transparency rather than using any paper notes. Also, if you use the card frames that are available to reinforce overhead transparencies, you can put additional notes on the frame, in sight to yourself but out of sight from the audience.

But a trainer does need to be skilful at using visual aids, so that they actually do reinforce learning. If you aren't slick when you are using visual aids, your ineptitude in handling them will often irritate participants. This can hinder learning in a big way.

Obviously there are some simple rules to follow when using visual aids.

- Firstly everyone in the training room should be able to easily see the visual aid. Participants shouldn't have to crane their necks or move their chairs to be able to see what you are showing them.

- Secondly, if there is sound involved with the visual aid – for example, a video – then every participant should be able to hear it. Neither should it be too loud, so that participants are in danger of being deafened or at least having a bad headache before very long.

Simple rules, but it is shockingly surprising how many trainers break these two basic rules and continue to use visual aids participants can't see, either because they are too small, in the wrong place in the training room, or simply written with orange or yellow marker pens onto flipchart paper. Or trainers who show a video through a small TV screen to a large group of participants; or use a poor recording where the volume won't turn up loud enough for participants to hear it, without the crackling noises that it makes drowning out the speech content.

All it needs to use visual aids well on a training course, is a certain amount of common sense. The best way to work out the benefits to the participants, of the visual aids that you are using, is to think about them from the participants' point of view. Some trainers get caught up in the technicalities of visual aids and forget why they are really using them.

Flipcharts

Of the three most used visual aids, flipcharts are something that most trainers couldn't do without. There is something comforting about a flipchart and stand, set next to you, in that lonely place the trainer occupies in front of the group. It is like your friend; some days it can feel like your only friend. It is also your symbol of power. You have the flipchart and marker pens, so surely you must be in charge. It doesn't always follow, but sometimes it's the nearest you will get to feeling that you are being assisted.

Flipcharts are very versatile. It is little wonder that most trainers favour them. The best type of flipchart stands to use are the free standing type. Although, there is always the possibility of tripping over the legs of the stand at some point during the training session, they are the most versatile. The benefits of having them free standing are outweighed by the dangers that they pose.

The type of flipchart that is attached to the wall can be difficult to use. If you aren't very tall, then turning the sheets of paper and putting them over the back of the frame, and getting them behind the flipchart, can be something that is worth selling tickets to watch. It is really not about the comedy value here, but the distraction you can cause as you fight with each sheet of paper. It is sometimes better to just tear each sheet off the pad as you have finished with it. Unfortunately you can then be left standing knee deep in sheets of paper. Not an attractive sight, especially for any participant who is interested in conservation issues – especially those involved in saving trees or the planet or both.

Also, using the type of flipchart that is attached to the wall is often very difficult for left-handed people. Most training rooms are set up for right-handed people. The flipcharts that are attached to the wall can sometimes be in a position that means a left handed person can't get to the side they need to be at, to be able to write on them without turning their backs to the participants.

Some of these flipcharts will slide along the runner on the wall, on which they are fixed, in which case a left-handed trainer can move them to the other side of the room. However, often the screen for the overhead projector pulls down at the side where the left-handed trainer needs to have the flipchart, making it impossible to get the flipchart in the right place.

With a free-standing type of flipchart you can place it where you want it to use it, so whether you are right handed or left handed, it can be in the best place for you to use. You can also get it closer to the group with which you are working; doing this can develop a more intimate feeling within the group.

It is preferable to have two flipchart stands and pads, in the same training room when you are running a course, (and one in each small group room that you will be using). If you have two flipcharts in the training room, then you can keep information displayed on one whilst you still want to refer to it, or whilst you add to this information using the second flipchart, so the group can see all the information at the same time. It also gives you more space to display feedback sheets from small group work, if you want to continue the discussion after the small group exercise has finished. It can save a lot of time moving flipchart sheets from one place to another, when you want to refer to them. It makes your presentation look slicker.

Having flipcharts and marker pens in each group room that you will be using for small group work means that participants will have some of the resources ready to use, when they move to these rooms to carry out exercises. This can save time in taking pens and paper into the rooms. The main advantage of using flipcharts as a visual aid is that they are a very versatile piece of equipment. You can record points on them, as you are making them to the group. You can expand on the point, if you or someone in the group has thought of something else, this then can be written on the flipchart. They can be used to write up instructions for an exercise so participants can refer back to them; you can write up reminders for the group; you can write up salient points or reminders of things that need to be discussed later on the course, as they come up.

They are a dynamic piece of equipment, you can quickly record something, draw a diagram or a picture to illustrate a point, or get a participant to write or draw something to illustrate their point.

However you can also pre-prepare flipchart sheets in advance, so that you can save some time when you are giving participants your pearls of wisdom. Then they don't have to wait for you to write it down as well.

Disadvantages

The disadvantages of using flipcharts are firstly, as has been said before, that you can trip over the legs when you are gliding elegantly and professionally across the floor of the training room. However as long as you don't do it too often, it can give you the 'human touch'. It can also give participants something to laugh at and can liven up a session. It tends to be an activity that is not to be recommended, but will not change the course of world events if you do happen to trip up.

Additionally, if you have got very poor handwriting, it can look really terrible, when magnified to the size it needs to be on a flipchart: and if you can't write in straight lines along the sheet, it looks even worse. Also if your spelling is poor, this doesn't help matters.

Lastly, once flipcharts have been written on and used with a group they tend not to be reusable. Even if you roll them up carefully, they still look tatty the next time you get them out, having crumpled edges and a tendency to roll up on themselves.

There are simple rules to follow for getting the most out of using flipcharts as a visual aid.

Position

You need to place the flipchart somewhere, where everybody in the group can see it. Be aware of the participants sitting nearest to you, and therefore near to the flipchart. You can easily get in between them and the flipchart, so that they can't see it. Check, at intervals, that everybody can see what you are writing and what you have written. Most trainers have a tendency to wander about, often, in front of the flipchart, so be careful when you move about the room. Make sure that you regularly look around the room to make sure everybody is looking comfortable. If in doubt ask the participants if they can all easily see the flipchart. If they can't, then you can adjust it.

Make sure you are in the best position to be able to write on the flipchart. Simple rule of thumb; if you are right-handed, then place the flipchart to the left of yourself. If you are left-handed place the flipchart to your right. This way you can write on it without covering what you are writing with your body.

Clarity

When you are writing on a flipchart, make sure you use marker pens, and make sure that the pens are fully working and are not the sort that squeak when you use them. Use colours that don't reflect too much light. Black, dark blue, dark green and dark purple are the best colours. Use red for highlighting, or underlining, or drawing attention to a point. Don't use it too much as a lot of red can be difficult to read. Don't use yellow, orange, pink or any of the pretty colours. They all reflect too much light. You will be able to read what you have written from where you are standing, right next to the flipchart, but the participants won't be able to read what you have written from where they are sitting.

Fat wax crayons for children are very good to use on flipcharts as they have bright colours, never leak or dribble, do not squeak – and you can keep a few in your pocket without fear of staining.

Be neat and tidy

Make your handwriting as clear as possible. If you have trouble writing in straight lines, buy the flipchart paper that is printed in squares, (like large squared graph paper). If you can't buy this, then either carry a couple of sheets that you have managed to get hold of, around with you, to use as a guide sheet. Or you can make you own, by ruling up a sheet of plain flipchart paper. You then put this sheet under the one that you are about to write on, holding it in place with sticky tack or masking tape. The same way as you use a guide sheet when using a letter writing pad of plain paper.

If you are concerned about spelling certain words that you either don't know how to spell, and never will do, no matter how hard you try, or words that you think will come up during the session, write them onto the flipchart before the session. You can then refer to them as needed, without anyone knowing. If you write the words using very small letters and a soft pencil, the participants can't see the writing. You can also use this technique to write up information that you are concerned about remembering. It makes your presentation look much more slick, if you don't have to refer to your notes when you are talking and of course when you get the spelling right as you are writing up on to the flipchart.

Make it slick

When you have finished talking about what you have written on the flipchart, then you always need to get rid of it, usually by turning over to the next sheet. For some reason, participants often find what you have written much more interesting than what you have moved on to talk about. They could be analysing your handwriting or checking your spelling. Don't give them the opportunity; always turn over when you have finished with that particular piece of information. If you have pre-prepared sheets on your flipchart pad, then leave a blank sheet between each prepared sheet. So when you turn over then you are turning over to a blank sheet and not giving participants an opportunity to read what you are going to cover next.

If you are intending to refer back to any of the information that you have written on to the flipchart sheets, on a later session on the training course, fold a corner on the bottom of the flipchart sheet when you have turned it over. If you write on the folded corner, what the sheet is about, you will be able to easily find it when you want to refer back to it later on in the training course. This saves all the noise, annoyance and inefficiency whilst you are training, finding the right place on the flipchart pad.

Don't over-use

Even though flipcharts are very versatile and easy to use, don't over-use them. Don't write down everything that you say, or that the participants say. Don't write in full sentences; just write down the main points or key words from any discussion. Remember you are recording things onto the flipchart to aid the participants' learning and retention of the subject that you are covering, not as a record of everything that has been said.

Finally, don't waste paper. Some participants object to how many trees that are being sacrificed by trainers because of the amount of paper that they can get through in one training session. It is quite acceptable to draw a line across a sheet of flipchart paper, if you have only used the top portion and you want to move onto something else, or to turn the pad over and use the other side. For some participants, seeing a trainer write one word on to a sheet of flipchart paper and then turn over can be very upsetting and annoying. You are doing you best not to upset or annoy anyone, so why do it over such a small thing.

Overhead projectors and Powerpoint presentations

One of the other benefits of flipcharts that hasn't been mentioned is that they don't require any power supply. Overhead projectors, Powerpoint presentations and videos all require a power supply. Overhead projectors and Powerpoint also require a blank screen on which to project the images that you are using. These things might sound so absolutely obvious, however it is easy to forget to take an extension lead with you. The room where you are running the training session, most certainly will have power, but it doesn't always mean that the equipment you want to use will actually reach the power source, from the place where it needs to be so that all the participants can see comfortably.

There is also the problem of the screen that you will need to use on which to project your images. The added problem will often be where to put the screen. These are very large pieces of equipment with feet that stick out quite a way, and can therefore be difficult to position. Sometimes the organiser of the course you are to run, will tell you that you can project onto a wall. This is perfectly acceptable, but you need to make sure that the wall isn't covered in wallpaper with large red roses or something similar, all over it. Or the wall isn't hung with pictures, usually the large framed variety, that can't be taken down. These sorts of walls are absolutely no good at all to project on.

The main advantage of using an overhead projector is that you can prepare your overhead transparencies and use them again and again. This obviously saves time and effort in the preparation for training courses. Unlike flipchart sheets they can go into your filing cabinet to be brought out the next time you run the course. They also don't take up much room and are easy to transport.

They are ideal when being used with large groups, to enable all the participants to see the points that you are making. They are actually not too good for working with small groups, in fact they work much better with large groups than small groups. With small groups who are often in a small room, the overhead projector can get in the way, obstructing the participant's view of the transparency itself. It can also obstruct the participant's view of you. You might find yourself having to move the overhead projector out of the way when you are not using it.

They were actually invented to be used with large groups in lecture theatre type places. However they are useful, if you have the space in the training room, and a good screen. You can display complex diagrams and use colour on your transparencies to make them more interesting. You can build up ideas using overlaid transparencies, which give participants an easy understanding of the concept of the idea you are trying to get across.

It is also easy to maintain eye contact with the participants when you are using an overhead projector – that is, if you are using it correctly. A great many trainers seem to have a need to stand facing the screen, reading from it, rather that reading from the actual transparency that is on the flat bed of the machine. Reading from the screen means that you will be turning your back on your audience. This is not the correct way of doing it.

Another disadvantage in using an overhead projector is that they can stop working. Bulbs can blow, or there could even be a power cut. The rule is never to totally rely on a visual aid. Always make sure that you could carry on the training session without it.

When using an overhead projector, these are the things to consider.

Position
Make sure that the overhead projector is placed so that the arm of the machine doesn't block the screen. All of the participants need to be able to see the whole of the transparency, without ducking and diving around in their seats.
Also, make sure that you can see the transparency that you are displaying clearly enough for you to be able to read it from the distance you are standing from the machine. You

cannot stand close to the machine, unless you are in a large room and you are projecting your transparency high onto the screen. If you stand close to it in a small room you will probably be blocking the view of your participants.

If you can't easily read what is on the transparency that you are using, either memorise it, (this always feels a bit stressful), or have a paper copy to hand. You will no doubt know what is on the slide, off by heart, but it is comfortable to have a back-up for those amnesia moments which all trainers suffer from occasionally.

Content

Don't overload your transparency with information and then read it out word for word. No doubt the participants can read as well as you can. They can also read more quickly than you can speak, so they will have got to the end of the transparency before you. They will be waiting for you to catch up with them. This method hardly keeps their interest in you or in the subject. This is actually a form of torture for participants, commonly called 'death by overhead projector'. If you have ever been subjected to it, it does actually feel like a slow death.

The rule of thumb is to try and keep to only three pieces of information on each transparency. Do not copy large amounts of text. Use the points that you have got on the transparency to expand upon. What you have printed on the transparency are useful prompts to you and as they will be the key points for the area on which you are working, and they will assist the participants in making their notes and aid retention of the key points.

Quantity

Don't use too many transparencies. Talking to one after another can be very tedious for the participants who have to listen to you. Use them only when you feel that they will aid participants' learning. Switch off the machine when you have finished talking to each transparency, even if you are using one transparency after another. The fans on the machine can be very noisy, and the noise quite intrusive. Also remove each transparency when you have finished speaking to it, as the same rule applies here as to getting rid of flipchart sheets when you have finished with them. Participants will continue to read what is being displayed on the screen and possibly find it more interesting than what you are now talking about.

Managing the process

If participants are taking notes from the transparencies whilst you are talking, then maybe one participant will ask you if you can leave the slide on for a little longer, as they haven't finished taking notes. This is a nightmare request as really the answer has got to be 'no'. You can't leave the transparency on, for one person, if you have finished talking to that one, and were about to put the next one up and continue with the subject area. Otherwise, both you and the rest of the group will be waiting for that person. This is not particularly comfortable situation for anyone. It is a bit like the television presenters, who are told by their producers to fill in for 30 seconds and you can see them struggling to find something to say to fill in the gap. If you anticipate that participants will want to take notes when you are using the overhead projector, it is advisable to give them paper copies of each transparency, with spaces to take notes. You can then move at the speed of the group and not of an individual.

All that has been said about the use of overhead projectors applies equally to Powerpoint presentations. If you feel that the term death by overhead projector rings true then there is a slightly more painful way for participants to die of boredom, this death by Powerpoint presentation. These presentations can move up a league in their ability to bore participants on training courses. Powerpoint, in the hands of a good trainer, who knows what he or she is doing, is a really good training tool. In the hands of a trainer who just loves the technology of it all, it can become a nightmare for participants, suffering the bouncing ball syndrome. That is the over-use of the animated ball bouncing across the screen, headings to the slides whizzing out from the corners of the screen, or whatever else they can find in the file named 'clever animations', to add to their presentation.

This doesn't help participants' learning, which is what visual aids are meant to do. It can be quite eye catching the first few times that it is shown, but after that it can be more irritating than interesting for the participants. Powerpoint in the hands of the other sort of trainer who is more or less technologically incompetent, can also be a nightmare, as this trainer clicks the button too many times and the slides whiz past, never to be retrieved. This often results in the trainer spending a long time trying to find them again, instead of giving up gracefully and getting on with the training course. The rule of thumb with Powerpoint is use it sparingly, use it with all the considerations that have been listed for the good use of overhead projectors and be able to use it well.

Videos

Flipcharts and overhead projectors are simple and friendly visual aids for the trainer, when compared with attempting to show a video. If anything can go wrong with a video, it will.The most common problem for trainers when they are using videos is not being able to find the right channel through which to show it. This usually happens when the person for whom you are running the training session, has welcomed you into the training room and has then disappeared into the depths of 'never land' and can't be contacted for help. Of course you need to arrive at the venue, in plenty of time so that you can sort out these sorts of problems. You know you can work out which channel the video shows through, but when stress levels are rising it can be difficult to be as clever as you know that you can be, in calmer times.

Another problem with using videos is getting one that has the content that you really want and isn't just 'good enough', because you can't find anything that exactly fits the bill. Many training videos were made some years ago. Although the content may be good, the fashion in which the actors are dressed gives away the era in which the video was made. Unfortunately, participants may find it difficult to ignore these details and will often decide that it is not only the clothes that are out of date, but the information as well.

Disadvantages

The disadvantages of using videos often outweigh the advantages. You should only use a video on a training session if there is really no other way of displaying the situation you want to show participants. They should be used sparingly. Participants will often move into 'cinema' mode when you get the video out. That is they think that you are showing a video to entertain them, not to add to the learning process. When you show a video on a training course you can almost guarantee that you will have one comment of 'when's the ice cream coming round'.

Other disadvantages are that if you have quite a large group it can be difficult to find a large enough TV screen for them to watch it. For some reason, most training rooms have medium or small-screened televisions. Sometimes with good planning it is possible to arrange the training course so that you have half the group watching the video, in a separate room, whilst the other half of the participants are engaged in another activity. Then the activities can be swapped over, so both groups have seen the video, but in more comfort than trying to get everyone around the television.

Advantages

The advantages are that you can get a really true to life and three-dimensional account of what you want to show participants, into the training room. If you were using a case study exercise then the subject would be much more two-dimensional.

When using a video for training purposes you should consider:

Size

You must make sure that the size of everything involved is correct. The size of the room, the group and the television screen all have an impact when showing a video.

Relevance to the subject area

You must make sure that the content of the video is really relevant to the subject area you are working on. Being 'good enough' or almost right won't keep the interest of the participants. Participants are often not too good at or willing to make the connections between what you are showing them, if it isn't obvious, or they are not so willing to make it easy for you and make the connections.

Focus

You need to make sure that you just don't put the video on and ask the group to watch it. You must tell them why they are watching it; what exactly they should be looking for in the video and what you are going to ask them to do at the end of the video. It is best to either produce a worksheet with some questions for participants to answer either whilst watching the video or immediately afterwards, or write up what you want them to look for, or questions that you want answering, on to the flipchart. Either way participants can refer to it both during watching the video and afterwards.

Actual things

Often, it is very helpful to have as a visual aid the very thing you are talking about, whether it is a document or form, a set of books, a working example of a car engine, a live animal or a Ming vase. The group will benefit from being able to see the actual object and even handle it if this is acceptable (care with the Ming vase!). If your session is about a more cerebral topic or a policy or procedure, then an associated object such as a replica of a famous painting or a small statuette can act as a focus. One very experienced sales trainer uses a plastic skull as a conversational companion during parts of his sessions, causing amusement in the group as well as making the message more memorable.

Remember, visual aids are not there to replace you; you are using them to help participants to learn more easily and effectively. But when you are using them, make sure you are in absolute control of them, don't let them be in control of you.

Finally, remember that you yourself are a visual aid to the participants' learning. Remember what we said about your appearance. Also, bear in mind that your personality, performance standards, presentation skills and personal credibility are all powerful elements of the overall training experience for the people in your care.

10
Dealing with
Difficult Participants

... there is always one
on every training course

Most trainers who run training courses on a regular basis, come across 'difficult' participants. They come in different shapes and sizes, but often exhibit the same range of behaviours, in different degrees.

No training course is complete without a difficult participant. At least this is what they seem to think. Life can be hard enough for a trainer, without having to cope with difficult participants. The more experience that you have in the training arena, the more confident you will feel about dealing with these people. It gets easier with practice, but it is never a pleasant situation to be in.

When you are faced with a 'difficult' participant, or if you are unlucky, a group of them, you have to decide whether the problem is yours or it is the participants'. Is it you who finds the participants' behaviour annoying or is their behaviour really disruptive to the other participants and to the smooth running of the training course? Trainers all have their own Achilles' heel; that is, all trainers can have a low tolerance to certain types of behaviour. You need to be able to recognise where your lack of tolerance lies, and work on being able to better put up with it. That is not letting yourself get emotionally involved with the behaviour.

131

When dealing with difficult participants your goal is always to eliminate or minimise the behaviour of the particular participant or group of participants; to maintain the self-esteem of the particular participant or participants who are causing the problem and to avoid further disruption of the group's processes.

Participants must never feel that they are back at school and are being caught being naughty. If you treat participants in any way that reminds them of being back at school, you may find that they will actually turn into naughty school children. You then have a really difficult group on your hands.

There are several types of participant behaviour that you might find difficult to cope with.

Participants who talk excessively

There are people who have something to say in answer to every question you pose or something to add to any information you have given to the group. This behaviour can be useful in stimulating a group discussion, but can be a problem if the participant's contributions are excessive and result in other participants not being able to either get a word in at all or have trouble in putting forward their point of view.

Non-participating participants

A difficult participant might be the shy or withdrawn participant, who doesn't contribute to the discussions. A participant who is shy can be very different from a withdrawn person, in their motives for not joining in with the training session. You may have a participant in your group who is genuinely shy and finds it difficult to participate, especially in any large group discussions. These people usually don't like attention being brought to them.

It is important to distinguish between the genuinely shy person and a participant who is withdrawn. This can sometimes be done with careful observation of their body language. Shy people will often look as if they want to join in, but don't have the courage to do so. They are more likely to look more relaxed and join in more in small group work, and be the most comfortable working in pairs. In these situations they are likely to feel less vulnerable and exposed, as they would be working in a large group situation.

A withdrawn person is not usually shy. They are withdrawing themselves from the whole learning process, often refusing to interact with other members of the group, either overtly or covertly. There is usually a reason for this type of behaviour but it can be difficult to get to the bottom of it, and discover why they are behaving in this way. Their comments, when they do join in with the rest of the group, are often negative or non-committal. These comments will often give you the best clues as the why they don't want to be in the training room. Or they will give major signals with their body language that you can't ignore. For example, they pull their chair slightly out of line with the rest of the group. If your participants are sitting in a semi-circle, this can be very noticeable. Or they sit looking out of the window, when you or other participants are talking, or they look more interested in their notepad than what you or anyone else is saying. With a set of signals like this, you would have to be totally insensitive and unaware of your surroundings, to miss them.

Unco-operative participants

Then you have the participants who are unco-operative. These participants are more forceful than those who are withdrawn. The withdrawn person, if not challenged, will often ride it out to the end of the course, write negative comments on the evaluation form, usually omitting to sign it, and leave. Unco-operative people will make you notice them, by either directly questioning what you are asking the group to do, or moaning whilst they are working on any exercise – usually in a loud voice, so that everyone can hear what they are saying.

The side conversationalists

In addition to all these types of behaviour of 'difficult' participants there are those who insist on talking to each other, usually when you are talking, or other participants are putting forward an idea or asking a question. These can often, but not necessarily, be participants who know each other, perhaps from the same organisation. Often they have arrived at the training course together and insist on sitting next to each other for as much time as possible.

The know-it-all

Then you have the 'know it all'. The participant who literally knows everything about the subject area on which you are working or at least thinks that they do. Everything you say, they have heard before, or want to discuss it from a different angle, that isn't appropriate to the particular course that you are running. Every example you give they have done it or done something better.

So, how can you deal with these difficult participants? With a bit of luck, you won't get all of them on the same training course, but that is always a possibility. Unfortunately there isn't a simple solution to dealing with difficult participants or difficult behaviour. It is usually a matter of thinking on your feet and doing the best that you can in that situation.

But when you are trying your best to deal with a participant who is being 'difficult' then you must remember that your objectives are to minimise the difficult behaviour, whilst maintaining the self-esteem of the individual participant.

The following are some tried and tested ways of dealing with difficult participants. You will need to develop your own repertoire that you can call upon when you need to.

Dealing with difficult participants

The excessive talker

The excessive talker can be assisted to lessen their contribution to the group by gently interrupting them and then asking them to summarise what they are saying; or asking them to put forward the key points of their contribution. As soon as you have got the summary or key points, move on to some one else. Either by inviting some one else to speak, by saying their name or by inviting a general contribution from the group. You also need to reinforce this with your body language, to show that you have moved on and want a contribution from some one else. Break eye contact with the difficult participant and turn away, slightly. This is a clear way of telling the participant that their contribution time is finished, and the focus has moved on to someone else.

If you are really struggling to shut up a participant or you are unfortunate enough to have a few participants with the same need to talk, then establish a procedure whereby each person contributes under a set of rules. There are various training techniques that can help in these situations.

The shy or the withdrawn participant

The structured techniques for managing discussion can also help when you have either shy or withdrawn participants on a training course. With the shy person it gives them the space to contribute, hopefully without feeling they are being put on the spot. With the withdrawn person, it gives a structure that forces them to contribute. It can even get them warmed up and making contributions, willingly.

If you have really shy people on your course it can help if you approach them at break time and talk to them. Be friendly with them and sympathetic to their difficulties in contributing, try and get to know them a little better. Then, when you are running the sessions, attempt to include them, particularly when you know that they know something about the subject under discussion.The same applies to the withdrawn person. Talk to them privately and find out what is the problem. Perhaps they have been 'sent' on the course by their manager and resent the fact. Maybe they feel that they already know the subject area that you are covering on the course. Speaking to them privately and perhaps sympathising with them can sometimes get them on your side, which will often improve their behaviour.

The unco-operative person

This technique can also work with the unco-operative participant. In most cases if you can get the foot of the problem that is causing the participant to exhibit difficult behaviour then you will be able to attempt to solve the problem. If you can't get to the bottom of why they are behaving in an unco-operative manner then at least you can discuss the need for them to be co-operative within the group, whilst recognising their particular feelings and needs.

The last resort with the unco-operative participant is to ask them to leave the training course. If they will really not co-operate with you and the rest of the group, then it is better for everyone if they leave the course. Remember that the group comes first and just occasionally an individual must be sacrificed for the sake of the group being able to learn. This is not a pleasant thing to have to do for any trainer, but you will often find that the rest of the group will thank you for your action. They will have being looking to you to provide the leadership in these difficult situations, and will expect you to deal with the situation.

It is your responsibility as a trainer to make sure that the group is comfortable and able to learn in a comfortable environment. They will not thank you for allowing a difficult situation to continue which is making them feel uncomfortable.

The side conversationalists

Then there are those participants that talk when you or other participants are talking. This can be very irritating to the other participants, as well as the trainer. It can also be distracting and make it difficult for participants to hear what is being said by those who are actually discussing the course content, and not having their own conversation.

The problem in dealing with this type of behaviour is that you can come over as appearing to be behaving like a 'teacher', catching pupils talking in class. So deal with this problem, carefully. The comment 'would you like to share what you are talking about with the rest of the group' can go down like a lead balloon in most situations.

You can try splitting the offending participants up from each other. Discretely, of course, otherwise you will sound like the teacher with naughty pupils again. You can split up participants by dividing the large group into smaller groups, making sure that the 'offenders' are in different groups. Then when the exercise has finished leave the groups sitting together, instead of inviting them to come back to their original seats.

If you weren't due to split the larger group into smaller groups, then change your plan and put in a quick exercise, or ask participants to discuss something in twos or threes, whatever formula that will split up the 'offending' participants.

Or ask the participants who are talking if they are okay. Giving them the benefit of the doubt, that maybe they haven't understood something, or maybe even the person who is doing the talking doesn't feel very well. The best way to do this is, if possible, is to move near to the people who are talking. This gets their attention more easily. Otherwise they could be so busy talking that they don't hear your caring comment.

Participants who are on a parallel universe

This type of participant isn't as difficult as the others are to deal with. However, as they seem to be inhabiting another planet or to be part of a parallel universe, they can be difficult to keep on track, with the course proceedings. They are usually keen, but introduce entirely irrelevant thoughts, or when working in small groups on an exercise can bring in irrelevances that confuse the rest of the group and take them off track. So the small group has to take so long sorting out what this particular participant means that it slows them down so much they don't get the exercise finished on time. With this type of participant, you just need to monitor what is happening and make sure that they don't take the other participants off track.

When you are dealing with difficult participants on a training course, it can seem a lonely place. There at the front of the participants, all on your own, feeling the rest of the group's anticipation of what you are going to do and an expectation that you will solve the problem. You can only do your best. Sometimes you will get it right and sometimes what you try won't work. Remember, this is a job you are doing. If you were serving customers in a hotel, you wouldn't be able to please everyone. The same is true when you are running a training course. You must do you best, but that is all you can do.

11
Presenting a Session

... standing and delivering

You will often be asked to give a presentation or lecture because you are known to possess certain knowledge and skills as well as an ability to put it over to other people. This is good and correct, but no matter how good you are at your own professional area of skills, there are many pitfalls to face if you are to become a trainer in that field. This chapter looks briefly at the business of getting up on your feet and presenting a session where you are the main resource and the learners will be invited to listen to your words and then, possibly, launch into discussions or exercises as described elsewhere in this book.

The process falls into two broad areas, similar to most of the techniques we have examined already. **Preparation** and **presentation** are the key areas for consideration.

Preparation

As before, take good note of the requirements of the course, the desired outcomes and the nature and composition of the learners' group. This is essential practice whatever you are doing as a trainer - not to consider these elements amounts to professional arrogance.

Let us work through the processes by using a recognisable and sensible example - a case study, if you like. Let's imagine you have been asked to present a session on a topic close to your heart and one which you know a great deal about. This topic is 'presentation skills'. You have been asked to make it a 45-minute session, with an additional half-hour to take questions and comments.

Do remember that the preparation is not a five-minute job, nor should it be left until the night before you are due to 'go on stage'. Any lack of preparation will be very obvious to your audience and they will be unforgiving if you louse it up for them.

The preparation should follow clear stages.

● Gather together all the information you can about your topic. This can come from several sources:

  • your existing experience and personal knowledge of the subject
  • material you have garnered from other people's work or teaching
  • books and magazines that have useful references to the subject
  • presentations you have made in the past on this or related topics.

● Read through the material once again.

● Find a quiet spot and an uninterrupted hour, a flipchart and a good pen. Write down on the chart every single idea that comes into your head around the subject of presentations, at random and without censoring yourself as you go along, for strange or illogical thoughts. Write everything. If you write each idea on a post-it note, this will make later analysis much easier. Keep at it until your mind goes empty.

- Carefully and analytically, go through all the random ideas and pick out the half dozen or so really key ideas that might form the backbone of your presentation. Mark these clearly (if on post-its, then rearrange them around the outside of the sheet). Then check all the other ideas, and mark them or re-position them around the key ideas. Even the less clever or less useable ideas should be allocated.

- When you have several groups of ideas, take another flipchart page and list the sub-topics with their associated ideas. Then decide which would be the best order to present these sub-topics to give a sound and comprehensive coverage of your subject. You now have the basis for your session - a route through the specific areas to be covered and a wealth of ideas for each one.

  Clearly you will not be able to mention every single idea you had in your ideas session, although you have listed them. Go through the lists and mark each item according to whether it is a 'must use', a 'should use' or a 'could use'. The musts are essential even if you only have two minutes to talk. The shoulds are important but could be condensed if necessary. The coulds are useful ideas if you have time or you find the group flagging. Overall, there should be far more individual points than you can properly use in the time available. That means that you will not dry up or look foolishly under-prepared.

- You now need to convert your flipchart into a useable crib for the session - you can hardly lay out a whole flipchart sheet to talk to. One favoured method is the spider diagram described in this book. Put your main topic (presentation skills) in the centre of a page and make the key areas that you identified the main legs, adding the sub-sub-topics appropriately. Use only key words - never sentences or long phrases. If you refine the spider until you are confident that it contains enough key ideas for you to cover in the allotted time, then you have a great crib to work from. Generally this will be sufficient for you (you do, after all, know a great deal about presentation skills anyway, and this will act as a reminder as you talk).

It has the added advantage of being a single sheet of paper rather than a droppable pack of cards, and you can work your way round the sequence moving from leg to leg. Also, you can see where you are going next and where you have just been, so any small interruptions can be easily dealt with.

• A final preparation trick is to try the presentation or lecture out on a friendly audience - surprising how often family or friends are dragged in for this essential rehearsal.

Presentation

Here is the real test - standing up and delivering your material. However, you have prepared well and well in time too. There are a number of particular aspects of presentation that you must consider - and continue to take note of as you are doing the actual delivery:

• position and stance
• speed and volume of speech
• use of notes
• gestures, mannerisms and body language
• use of humour
• use of microphones
• using the audience and eye contact
• opening, middle and closing
• taking comments from the group

Position and stance

Make sure you check the resources and facilities before you start the session. Have you got a table to work from, a lectern or just a chair? Where are the audience in relation to where you are expected to be? Is there a stage or dais that you will have to be on? Will this make you more remote from the group?

Are there suitable power sockets? Check the ideas from elsewhere in this book - setting up a lecture or presentation is no different from setting up an exercise or a led discussion.

If you know these factors, you can tailor your session to fit. You can decide how mobile you will be. You may need to keep fairly close to where your notes are or to the overhead projector if you are using images. The group may be put off your presentation if you rush up and down like a caged lion, or equally if you are totally static and only moving your mouth. Choose a style of presentation that you are comfortable with, whilst maintaining audience attention and interest.

Look the part. Do not slouch or keep your hands in your pockets. Be animated by all means but think how you appear to the group. They must have a good impression from the start.

Speech and volume

It is quite hard for new trainers to gauge just how fast or loud to talk. The clues are simple - everyone must be able to hear you, see you and understand you. Pitch you voice to suit the accoustic of the room and talk slightly more slowly that you would normally, without reducing it to an embarrassing drawl. Remember to pause occasionally to give the group time to absorb your words and take a short breather - about 6/7 seconds should do the trick.

Do not rush at breakneck speed from the beginning to the end. Try to make the audience move or shift their posture at least once every eight minutes or so. This is important to keep their attention. It can be done (a) with a piece of humour - nobody can laugh without wriggling a bit and changing position (try it!), (b) introducing a good visual aid or something you can pass round the group, (c) moving yourself to a different location so that the group have to turn to follow you or (d) involving them with a question or a two-minute talk-in-pairs exercise, great for keeping all the people on their toes.

Use of notes

Many trainers fall foul of notes. If you choose the spider diagram approach mentioned in preparation, you can use this as a basis for your session. The advantages are that you can leave it on the desk or lectern and no one knows it is there. You will seem to be a very confident and comprehensive speaker. Make the words on the diagram large enough to see from a couple of yards away - then you can move about a bit without having to take notes with you.

If you use cards or sheets of paper to talk from, there is a danger that you can become lost or confused if the sequence becomes upset. Have you ever seen a speaker drop his or her cards on the floor? Dreadful problem and the audience will not be sympathetic. Holding A4 sheets is also hard - if you are nervous, the pages will flutter as your hands are shaking - a sure sign to the audience.

Whatever system you choose, make the notes:

- legible from a distance
- crisp and short
- highlighting key words only

- identifying visuals or other aids when appropriate
- numbered and tabbed if on cards
- numbered if on pages.

Gestures, mannerisms and body language

Most people use gestures, hand-movements and facial expressions as they talk. There is no reason why you should not use yours when giving a talk. However, take care not to overdo it. The audience can become mesmerised by excessive gesturing. Likewise, do avoid irritating mannerisms like jangling keys in your pocket or twiddling with pencils. When the audience starts to count your mannerism use, you have lost them as far as the topic is concerned.

Body language is a subject that demands a study of its own. You probably know quite a bit about it, as we have suggested already in the book. Use the ideas in both directions - make sure that you exhibit positive body language and watch the audience for signs of tiredness or loss of concentration.

Use of humour

This is a contentious subject. Some people can use humour, tell jokes or make a comic riposte - and some can't. If you cannot do it, don't try. If you can, then use it with restraint and caution. It is not good if the audience leave after your excellent session chuckling about your many jokes but not remembering a word of your text.

There are obvious topics and types of jokes to avoid - this can be determined by a careful assessment of the audience and the organisation that hired you, together with your own sense of good taste and propriety. Never joke about race, gender, religion, disability or disaster - never.

Use of microphones

If the group you are talking to is large, the organisers may offer you a microphone. This could be one of three types, stand, hand-held or button. The last two could be radio mikes. In any case, there are a few useful tricks.

Hand-held mikes are a pain, because they need to be held at a fairly fixed distance from your face in order to produce a consistent sound level. This means that, if you swing round, the mike has to move with you. If you momentarily forget and lower the mike out of range, the audience will be suddenly presented with a virtually silent speaker. Try and practice the necessary control, without an audience, before you are invited to speak with one.

Stand mikes necessitate your standing fairly still. This can be a great inhibition if you need to move about and use different visuals or other materials.

Button or head-mounted mikes are favourite because they do not inhibit movement and can virtually be forgotten throughout the session.

Do check any of these systems before the group arrives as your fiddling with a crackling or intermittent sound system is a great turn off for them, as you will soon find out.

Using the audience and eye contact

Just as you keep in eye contact with someone you are chatting with, so you need to keep in eye contact with your group. If fairly small, then you can rove around the group catching each person in turn. Do not linger too long on any one person - this can be intimidating or embarrassing. If the group is large - or if you are speaking in the Albert Hall - look at each section of the audience in turn. Each person will think you are looking straight at them.

If you need to talk to an individual, try to use a name (or ask for one if it is a stranger) and avoid concentrating on one individual to the annoyance of the rest.

Keeping in eye contact is essential for checking how well you are doing. You will soon spot someone who is losing concentration or who is engaged on some other activity. See the section on dealing with disruptions for further advice on this. You need to be in control, and looking your audience in the eye is a good way of doing this.

Opening, middle and closing

There is the old story of the preacher who was asked why people always seemed to remember his sermons. He said, 'First I tells 'em what I'm going to tell 'em, then I tells 'em, then I tells 'em what I told 'em - an' they don't never forget!' There is sense in this and you should identify the start, the main text and the close for your session. Once decided, you can allocate timings and then stick to them.

● A good opening should catch the group's attention and keep it. They must want to hear you and learn from you, Go in positive, encouraging and enthusiastic. If you have, say, six prime points, write them beforehand carefully on a flipchart and leave this in sight to act as an agenda and check list.

● The main body of the session should be in easily digested chunks - remember pauses, humour, change of emphasis - and must contain all the 'must use' items you identified in the preparation. It should also cover the 'should use' items too. If time permits, use the coulds as well. Leave a couple of smaller items in the plot to use if you need to fill in a couple of minutes at the end.

- The conclusion must also be positive and should be a swift run-through of your prime points - but should not add any new material. When you have finished, say so, thank the audience and either sit down or open the question session.

Taking comments and questions

This needs to be just as carefully time controlled as the presentation. Try to let as many questioners as possible have their say and do not let a lone know-it-all hog the time. If you do not know the answer to a question, then say so and promise to find an answer and send it on as soon as possible. Do not try and flannel your way through - someone there may know the right answer!

At the end of the question session, try and summarise very swiftly and again close positively. You might be invited back if the whole session was a great success!

12
Evaluating the Training and the Learning

... how was it for you?

The final part of any training intervention is the evaluation of both the learning and the actual training and the results for the organisation. The way in which you will carry out the evaluation should be planned at the same time as you are planning the training.

Evaluation is a process that involves the planned collection of information so that informed judgements can be made about the value or effectiveness of something, in this case the value of the training intervention to both the learners and the organisation. Measuring the value of the training isn't always an easy task, but it is important and should not be compromised because of the difficulties that might be involved. After all, considering the resources, the money, time and effort that are invested in any training event, evaluation makes good sense. Organisations need to know if their investment in the training process will make or has made any difference to their staff performance and ultimately to the performance of the organisation.

So, evaluation serves a number of purposes.

- It is to find out if the participants taking part in the training intervention feel that the learning outcomes have been achieved.

- It is to give participants an opportunity to give feedback on the content and style of the training, so that any necessary changes can be made to the style and content of the training intervention.

- It helps you as a trainer to become more aware of how your training style impacts on other people and what the actual impact is on the work of the organisation.

In any training intervention there are four types or levels of evaluation required:

- the evaluation of the actual training – **reaction evaluation**
- the evaluation of the learning achieved by the participants – **learning evaluation**
- the evaluation of the improvement of the participants performance in relation to their job role – **performance evaluation**
- the evaluation of the impact of the training on to the actual performance of the organisation – **impact evaluation.**

Some organisations only carry out an evaluation of the training, thinking that they are also evaluating the learning, and the impact on the organisation's results is forgotten. This type of evaluation is usually carried out immediately after the training intervention. The participants on the training course are asked to fill in an evaluation form, or a 'happy sheet' as they are affectionately called by some trainers, at the end of the course. These sheets address such things as the administration of the training, whether it was good, bad or indifferent, what they thought of the refreshments and the venue, and how well the trainer performed. The sheets usually contain questions about what the participant learnt, what they found interesting or useful, and whether the learning actually met their objectives for attending the course. Even if these sheets do ask learners to consider what they have learnt, it is not possible to get a true picture of what they have learnt at this stage.

Learning is usually defined as a change in behaviour. Participants who have attended training courses need to be able to try out their new knowledge, skills and/or attitudes back in the workplace to be able to know whether they have really learnt something or not. It is a bit like attending a training course to learn how to drive a car, sitting in a room being told about the theory of driving a car, maybe sitting in a mock up of a car and then being asked whether they have learnt how to drive. Some participants might feel that they have learnt to drive – however, they would no doubt be proved wrong if they attempted to take a car onto the road. They will have learnt something from being on the training course, but until they try it out it will be difficult for them to define exactly what this is. They would certainly know more about how to drive a car than before they attended the training course, but they would not be competent or confident in what their actual level of ability to drive a car, until they had tried it out. So, the evaluation of learning needs to come later,

The evaluation of learning usually takes place around 3-4 weeks after the training intervention has taken place. This timescale gives the learner enough time to try out what they have learnt in real life situations and therefore find out what they can and can't do and what they can and can't do better or more easily.

To find out what participants have learnt, you can use different methods to collect the information. The choice of the methods will often be led by the type of organisation with which you are working. The differences between organisations can often be summed up as one with formal structures and clear hierarchies or those that run in an informal way, with less structure and reporting and managerial hierarchies.

Whatever the type of organisation, you need to evaluate the learning against the learning outcomes that were developed for the training intervention. How you do this is the bit that will depend on the style of the organisation. In more formal and perhaps larger organisations, the evaluation can be done by questionnaires or through the existing structures of supervision. In the more informal organisation, you can still use questionnaires but they would probably be used to chat through what the learners have actually learnt and then completed together; with you and the learner having input into the finished ideas. In informal or smaller organisation you can observe what the learner is doing and discuss with them their improvements in how they are now undertaking their job, or more usually the part of the job, or the tasks that the training was designed to improve.

After you have looked at what the learners have actually learnt from attending the training intervention, you would need to move this into evaluating how an individual's performance has actually improved. This type of evaluation can be carried out at the same time as evaluating what a learner has actually learnt, as it is often difficult to separate out the two areas. In an example of staff being sent on a course to improve their selling skills, what they have learnt could be the persuasion skills to keep customers on the telephone in order to improve their ratio of getting appointments from cold calling potential customers. The evaluation of their performance would be looked at in how big the improvements have been to converting cold calls to appointments, measured against previous performance and new targets that have been set since the training intervention.

Lastly the impact evaluation would be evaluating the impact that the increased number of appointments that have been generated has had on the overall sales figures and the income to the business.

Evaluation is often an after-thought for some organisations, but should actually be at the forefront of their minds when any training is being planned. It can often be up to you as the trainer to lead the evaluation process. Do this well and you could become invaluable to the organisations for which you work.

Happy training!!!

Have fun and enjoy the privilege that you have in being able to meet so many different people on your training courses, all bringing with them new ideas and ways of looking at things that you can learn from and improve your knowledge and understanding as you go along.

Remember – learning is always a two-way process.

Index

Sahara Consultancy

Sandy Leong set up Sahara Consultancy 15 years ago to provide training and consultancy for the voluntary and not-for-profit sectors. Her specialist area is training for trainers. The Sahara Consultancy team of trainers deliver training across the UK and further afield to a wide range of organisations. The team have all been practitioners in their specialist areas and bring to the training situation hands-on knowledge and experience.

Sahara Consultancy run a wide range of courses, either as open programmes or bespoke training tailored to the needs of the individual organisation. All members of the Sahara team have their own specialist areas of interest.

Sahara Consultancy also produce training materials for these sectors that can be used by busy training specialists or those new to training, to deliver their own training sessions.

For further information, contact:

Sahara Consultancy
54 William Street, Loughborough, Leics., LE11 3BZ, UK
tel: (0044) (0) 1509 234628

Some comments about this book

When teaching prospective new teachers, it's very important not only to recommend indicative reading lists but ones that will clearly support the student in the initial learning stages. This book contains many areas that contribute to this thought in a manner that gives an even balance to the initial knowledge and experience of new learners.

The book is strong in 'differentiation' as a tool to classroom activity and course design.

We would very much encourage our students to refer to or acquire this book as reference material towards supporting requirements of self-development and assessment work.

Richard Swann, Loughborough College

After almost a lifetime of training, I often find that books on training are either too academic and theoretical, or concentrate on the technical details and ignore the human and affective side. I was pleased to see that this book concentrated on the human side of training; on the interaction with participants.

One of the intriguing aspects is the way in which the book itself acts as a model of the training process advocated. The author stresses the importance of enthusiasm right from the start and herself sets an excellent example in her own approach. The emphasis is on making the participants feel comfortable and the book achieves this itself by adopting a technique of direct speech which provides a feeling of spontaneity and candid contact between author and reader.

Throughout the book there is an awareness of the frailty of human endeavour and the need to accept that things will sometimes go wrong; the aim is to achieve a high standard, not necessarily perfection. Hence the sub-title 'A very practical guide'. This is not an academic book with references and notes; rather a basic support for the novice trainer and a refresher for the more seasoned practitioner.

Although its main strength will be in giving confidence to those who are uneasy about the prospect of facing an adult audience with all the problems that this entails, I found this book a welcome stimulus to questioning my own techniques and methods. It has made me think again; and that surely is the prime purpose of any book. After all, in the words of the naturalist Luther Burbank, 'It is well for people who think, to change their minds occasionally in order to keep them clean'!

Morry van Ments
President of the Society for Advancement of Games and
Simulation in Education and Training